HORST KRÜGER

Horst Krüger (1919–99) was a German journalist, novelist and travel writer. Published in 1966, *The Broken House* was critically acclaimed as an exemplary portrait of youth in Nazi Germany.

HORST KRÜGER

The Broken House

Growing Up Under Hitler

TRANSLATED FROM THE GERMAN BY
Shaun Whiteside

VINTAGE

1 3 5 7 9 10 8 6 4 2

Vintage is part of the Penguin Random House group of companies
whose addresses can be found at global.penguinrandomhouse.com

 | Penguin
Random House
UK

First published in Vintage in 2022
First published in the UK in hardback by The Bodley Head in 2021

First published in Germany as *Das zerbrochene Haus: Eine Jugend in
Deutschland* by Rütten & Loening in 1966
New edition published by Schöffling & Co. in 2019

penguin.co.uk/vintage

A CIP catalogue record for this book is available from the
British Library

ISBN 9781529113198

Printed and bound in Great Britain by Clays Ltd, Elcograf S.p.A.

The authorised representative in the EEA is Penguin Random House
Ireland, Morrison Chambers, 32 Nassau Street, Dublin D02 YH68

Penguin Random House is committed to a sustainable future for our
business, our readers and our planet. This book is made from Forest
Stewardship Council® certified paper.

Of course truth must be written
in a struggle with untruth
and it cannot be general, elevated, ambiguous.
For to be general, elevated, ambiguous
is precisely the nature of untruth.

Bertolt Brecht

A number of references in the text to German culture, history and politics, marked with an asterisk, are explained in the glossary at the back of the book.

CONTENTS

A PLACE LIKE EICHKAMP

Berlin is an endless sea of houses in which a stream of aeroplanes is forever drowning. It is a big grey stone desert that, without fail, excites me every time I float down towards it: Magdeburg, Dessau, Brandenburg, Potsdam, Zoo. They're building high-speed underground lines and urban motorways, they're developing sophisticated spaghetti junctions and rakish television towers. All of this is the new, modern Berlin, the technical merry-go-round of the rotating island city, propelled from within by the brittle, laconic wit of its people, and from without by capital. It is beautiful and radiant, this new Berlin, but it's not until I'm sitting on the suburban railway, now trundling through the West, the train quite empty and East-German shabby, that I actually feel at home. This is my Berlin, the roaring, singing trauma of my childhood, my paused tin toy, which still seems to be saying, with its bright and swiftly hammering tone: You're here, you're really here, it's always been like this and it will always be so. Berlin is a yellow polished wooden seat, hard and bare, a dirty, rain-drenched window, a compartment that smells ineffably of German trains. It's a mixture of stale smoke, iron and the bodies of countless workers coming from Spandau, margarine sandwiches in their bellies, who once upon a time, at fourteen, went to confirmation and read the *Morgenpost* every day after that.* All of that is Berlin and so is the dispenser on the draughty platform that delivers peppermints: white and green, wrapped in stiff silver paper. It's the slamming of the electric doors and the shout at Westkreuz station: 'Please stand back!' Nobody is surprised by that any more, nobody needs to stand back, but the shout is still there and the man with the signalling disc and then the sudden shove forward. Berlin is a shabby yellow ticket for fifty pfennigs. Even today you can travel from Spandau into the capital of the German Democratic Republic for fifty pfennigs.

I'm sitting on the suburban train on the way to Eichkamp. I know Eichkamp isn't what they would call a hot topic these days. People want to read articles on Berlin: Write us a piece on the Wall or the new Philharmonie, the Congresshalle or the Christmas market up there. That kind of thing is always in demand. But Eichkamp? What is it? What's that supposed to be? It doesn't feature on any list of sights in Berlin; no African politician and no American who's crossed the ocean to find the Kurfürstendamm delightful and the Wall appalling, is ever brought to Eichkamp. Eichkamp is basically nothing, just a small, insignificant housing estate between Neu-Westend and Grunewald, an estate like countless others on the margins of the big city, where the sea of houses gradually dissolves into the leafy countryside. In fact, Eichkamp is only a memory for me. It is the place of my childhood. It was here that I grew up, played marbles and hopscotch and tag in the streets and went to school and later came back from university to eat and sleep. Eichkamp is simply my home which – as a stranger – I want to see again after over twenty years.

I'm coming back as a citizen of the Federal Republic. Today I've left my job and my car, my own world over there; I'm returning all by myself, but not because I think it's touching and beautiful for a grown man to pursue the traces of his childhood. It's a repellent yearning in ageing men to pore over their childhoods: the obscenity of old men who crouch, hearts thumping, in playgrounds as if some secret Eden might be discovered there. For me Eichkamp wasn't paradise, and my childhood wasn't a secret dream. Eichkamp was simply my youth under Hitler, and I would like to see it again and understand at last what things were like under Hitler. Everything that was the Third Reich back then: the torchlight processions on Unter den Linden and the cheering on the radio and the rapture of renewal are all over, gone, forgotten. The bread ration cards and the bombs over Eichkamp and the Gestapo who sometimes came from the city centre in black limousines were forgotten long ago. Now, I think, we need to understand. Almost a lifetime has passed, the rapture and the depression have faded away, everything is new and different now. I come from the West, a citizen of the Federal Republic, I've come to Eichkamp because I am troubled by the question of what it was really like, the things none of us can understand any more. Now, I think, now we really need to understand.

At night my dreams have sometimes taken me back to Eichkamp. They are heavy, fearful dreams after which I sometimes wake up at six in the morning feeling shattered. Thirty years is a long time, the time of a generation, time to forget. Why can't I forget?

My dream: I've come to Eichkamp, I'm standing outside our house. Long cracks criss-cross the outside walls; our house has been damaged by fuel-air bombs. A small, two-storey terraced house on the edge of Berlin, quickly and cheaply built in the 1920s. Now it's been pitifully repaired. The doors and windows rattle, the wooden floor inside is crumbling. My mother sits in the study reading to my father

3

from a book. The room is small and low-ceilinged, and furnished in that indescribably dissonant way that was called bourgeois at the time: department-store junk, augmented by heirlooms from the good old days. A round pedestal table covered with a lace doily, a standard lamp with a cardboard shade, a cheap pine desk, sharp-cornered and studded with brass nails. An outsized chandelier hangs low in the room with its long crystal droplets: an heirloom from Buckow. A huge oak cabinet fills almost a third of the room: an heirloom from Stralau; 'our baroque cabinet', it was called at home. My father sits indifferently at his black-painted desk. As always he has files in front of him, and as always he is scratching his head, his 'wound': Verdun 1916. Behind the round pedestal table my mother sinks into a stained, fabric-covered armchair; 'our club chair', it was called. The light from the lamp falls softly on the book. Her hands are slender, her fingers long and delicate, and they dart nervously over the lines. She has Catholic eyes: dark, trusting, goitrous. There is something proclamatory in her voice. She is reading from a book that bears the title *Mein Kampf*. It is late summer 1933.

No, my parents were never Nazis. That's what makes the case so suspicious. They read this book by the new Herr Chancellor with the big, astonished eyes of children. They read it anxiously and expectantly: there must have been a massive amount of German hope in there. They had no other books, only the address book for Greater Berlin, the Bible and, admittedly, the popular novel *Jettchen Gebert*. Otherwise they listened only to Paul Lincke, *Frau Luna*, and so on, and on New Year's Eve *Die Fledermaus* at the Admiralspalast, and sometimes the request programme on the radio; at a pinch the overture to *Donna Diana*.* My parents were, in that touching way, 'apolitical', like almost everyone in Eichkamp in those days. In the twelve years under Hitler

I never actually met a real Nazi in Eichkamp. That's it, that's what's dragging me back. They were just upright, hard-working bourgeois families, a bit limited and narrow, lower middle class, with the horrors of the war and the anxieties of inflation behind them. Now they wanted peace. They had moved to Eichkamp in the early 1920s because it was a new island of green. There were still fir trees and Scots pines in the garden, and the Teufelssee was only a quarter of an hour away. Their children could swim there. They planned to grow vegetables in the garden. At the weekend they contentedly sprinkled the lawn. It almost smelled like the countryside. In the city the wild Golden Twenties were already under way. People were doing the Charleston and even starting to tap-dance. Brecht and Eisenstein were beginning their triumphal ascent.* The newspapers reported street fights in Wedding, battles on the barricades outside the trade union building. That was a long way away from us, we could have been separated by centuries. Repellent, incomprehensible instances of agitation. In Eichkamp I learned at a young age that a respectable German is always apolitical.

A strange feeling as the train now pulls into Eichkamp station. Remembering, forgetting, remembering again, the changing times: what is this? What you're doing now isn't new, you've experienced it before, it was always like that: rise from the yellow polished seat, take down your belongings from the netting, push your way past strangers, grip the brass handle on the door, thumb around the top, then slowly pull the handle to the right, open the door. A brave feeling. As the train speeds hard to the edge of the platform, step right to the front and the airstream suddenly blows in your face, and then, as the carriage goes on trundling slowly along, you feel that terrible temptation to jump off. I know it's forbidden, it says so above the door, and it was forbidden even back then, under Hitler, but now once again I feel that temptation that appealed to me so much when I was in my third year at school: if you jump off at the right moment, and catch your body's centrifugal force right with your feet, the same momentum will carry you up the steps in Eichkamp station, you'll be first to the barrier, first out into the green square, first along the narrow garden path leading to the estate.

The Eichkampers follow behind you at a leisurely pace. A few gentlemen with briefcases: inspectors, office clerks, officials. Elderly women who have been shopping in Charlottenburg or at Zoo, and who are now struggling, with waddling gait and in dresses with big floral patterns, towards little houses somewhere. Young girls who have come here to visit their aunts. Lads with football boots under their arms, who immediately turn to the right because that's where the sports fields are. In the old days they sometimes wore blue shirts. Those were the Jewish boys who came to play at the Zionist pitch here in Eichkamp.

What is time? What is memory? How can it be that you're doing all these things again as if you were fourteen? Four years of primary school in Eichkamp, nine at the Grunewald grammar, nine years jumping daily from the suburban train and meanwhile the swastika flying over Eichkamp; first scepticism and then the upbeat mood we had because we were doing so nicely again. The Katzensteins and the Schicks and the Wittkowskis had moved away. No one had really noticed, in fact. They were our good Jews: the bad ones lived around Alexanderplatz.

Every Eichkamper had at least one good Jew. My mother preferred Jewish doctors. 'They're so sensitive,' she used to say. Arnold Zweig lived in Eichkamp at the time. His fashionable flat roof was un-German and had to be given a Teutonic gable after he fled. Ludwig Marcuse lived three houses away from us, and he too had left in 1933. Nobody noticed any of this. Elisabeth Langgässer lived next door. She sometimes came to our house to listen to Beromünster. She always said that Hitler would have gone to the wall in three or four months' time. It was obvious. She went on believing that for twelve years. And stayed until the end.*

And then came the day of the first food ration cards, 1 September 1939. I'm standing outside the grocery shop and can no longer buy what my mother wanted. Butter is rationed, and you need cards to swap for bread. The Eichkampers look morose. Isn't it just like it was back in 1917? Then the first planes. I stand in the garden and hear three English ones growling high in the sky. Frau Langgässer steps up to the fence. She is small, squat, wearing French-style make-up and horn-rimmed glasses. When she walks down our street the children call after her: 'Here comes the paint-box! Here comes the paint-box!' And Frau Langgässer says to me: 'These are our liberators, Horst, believe me,' and she looks critically up into the sky with a short-sighted squint. And then later all the heavy bombs over the estate and then the Russians who fired their guns here too and also broke into houses and said: 'Woman, come!' Had Eichkamp deserved that? Then the British came and the years of hunger, the patched-up little houses, the time of the lovely heyday of the black market, the currency reform and the blockade and then the city's slow recovery.

It's curious: Eichkamp stands here now just as it did before. It's as if hardly anything had happened, as if it had all just been a horrible episode, a nightmare, an oversight of history. That oversight was repaired long since. The old terraced houses, with a few new bungalows dropped shyly in between them. The old houses are tall and narrow, the walls rendered with yellowish mortar and Virginia creeper running up them. The gardens, the gardens of Eichkamp – do they still count as Berlin? Here the lilac blooms again in heavy umbels, bluish purple and white, a scent of jasmine flows from the front gardens. Gladioli stand bolt upright in beds and beside them strawberries and onions, dill for the kitchen, lettuces, kohlrabi, red cabbage and chervil, pine trees in the background and the Brandenburg spruce with their tall, narrow, springy trunks. The radio tower is there too, and somewhere there is lime blossom. 'Sweet is the immortal scent of the lime-trees,' as the poet wrote. Didn't I first read that in Eichkamp?

But I'm getting sentimental. Of course: I'm on my way home. And as always when you come home after decades everything is looking smaller and smaller now, the houses, the gardens, the streets – how could one even live behind such tiny windows? And Schmiedt the butcher is still selling his sausages and his mince, he must be ancient, and Labude the baker is still there, or at least his shop is, they survived too. I always used to go there to buy five-pfennig 'snails', they were small, round, spiral-shaped sweet buns, and at the weekend I was allowed to buy cream cakes: four pieces for ten pfennigs. That was our Sunday coffee treat.

I walk on as I did back then: Fliederweg, Lärchenweg, Buchenweg, Kiefernweg, Vogelherd, Im Eichkamp – all narrow, dainty little streets, still without pavements even today, tiny houses with narrow front gardens, green shutters on the old-fashioned windows and behind them only upright, respectable people who tend to their craft, their business and their study. Eichkamp was the world of good Germans. Their horizon extended as far as Zoo and Grunewald, Spandau and Teufelssee – but no further. Eichkamp was a little green cosmos. What business did Hitler have here, in fact? Here they voted only for Hindenburg and Hugenberg.*

And then, all of a sudden, I've arrived. But there's nothing there, just a hole: gravel, rotten wood, broken stones, a lot of sand and greenery growing over it. There's a battered suitcase down in the basement. A basement, overgrown, run to seed, forgotten – left over from the big war, a ruined remnant of the battle for Berlin, a ruined house of the kind that you can find beside the radiant, matter-of-fact new buildings. There are empty spaces like this everywhere, white patches on the atlas of our new German affluence. The owners are dead or missing, they're living abroad, they've forgotten the world that was, they don't want to be reminded of it. And I stand there and think: So this is your past, this is your legacy, this is what they've left you with. This is where you grew up. It was your world. The ground plan barely covers thirty square metres: our house once stood here, two storeys high and topped by another pitiful attic room for the maid. And you were brought to these thirty square metres in 1923 as a three-year-old, and the last time you stepped inside this house you were twenty-four, and a German lance corporal in 1944. You had come back from the front in Italy. You were carrying a petrol can holding twenty litres. You brought twenty litres of olive oil back from the war, and when we had eaten the fried potatoes made possible once again by this precious oil we all fell ill. We threw up. The fat was too much. We simply had to vomit. We – at the time that meant: my parents and I. My sister had already killed herself in 1938.

So I'm back home. I'm in Eichkamp. I'm standing by our property, the lime trees are in bloom again, and I think that if I could understand right now what had happened in this house, I would know what it was like back then – all that stuff with Hitler and the Germans. Somewhere in Charlottenburg there must be a land registry office, you must be on the list. It's indisputable. You still own a ruin, this basement, and if you could remember, then the house would stand once more: this colourless, bleak, terrible lower-middle-class house whose son you are. I'm a little ashamed to come from this poky, washed-out lower-middle-class house; I would like to be the son of a scholar or of a lowly workman. I wish I was Thälmann's son or Thomas Mann's, then I'd have been born on the front line, but I only come from Eichkamp.* I'm a typical son of those harmless Germans who were never Nazis and without whom the Nazis would never have been able to do their work. That's the point.

Remember, remember: how are you supposed to remember everything? My earliest memory of Hitler is one of people cheering. I'm sorry to admit it, because these days historians know otherwise, but speaking for myself, all that I heard at first was cheering. It didn't come from Eichkamp. It came from the radio. It came from the far-off, foreign city of Berlin, it came from Unter den Linden and the Brandenburg Gate, a twenty-minute journey from Eichkamp by suburban train. That's how far away it was.

It was a cold January night, it was a torchlight procession, and the radio announcer, who was actually singing and sobbing in a loud voice more than he was reporting, must have been experiencing something tremendous. There must have been incredible cheering on the grand boulevard of the Reich capital, and all well-intentioned people, all real, young Germans must have poured into the city, from what I could hear, to pay homage to the elderly Field Marshal and his young Chancellor.* They were both standing at the window. It must have been something like a Hallelujah from the redeemed: Berlin, a joyful celebration; Berlin, a springtime fairy tale of the nation. There was chanting and marching and shouting and roaring and then again the sobbing voice on the radio singing something about Germany's awakening and repeating like a refrain that now everything, everything was going to change.

The people of Eichkamp were sceptical. My parents heard it all with surprise and a hint of fear. Somehow so much happiness and greatness didn't fit inside our cramped dwelling, our rooms crammed full of all kinds of junk and knick-knacks. Shortly after eleven my father turned the radio off and went to bed slightly perplexed. What was happening? What worlds were there outside? But the elderly Field Marshal and his young Chancellor, the latter often in evening dress, and what would from now on be called the Cabinet of National Concentration, later descended upon Eichkamp too – like hope. The sceptics grew calmer, the unconvinced more reflective, the small businesspeople optimistic. Suddenly the storm of the great world had crashed into this small green oasis of apoliticals, not a storm of politics, more of a spring storm, a storm of German rejuvenation. Who wouldn't want to set sail in that?

The black, white and red flags that the people of Eichkamp had always chosen in preference to the black, red and gold were now joined by swastika flags, in large numbers, big and small, often home-made flags with a black swastika on a white background. Some people in their haste had sewn the swastikas on the wrong way round, but their good intentions were plain to see. It was the time of renewal, and one day my mother came home with a little triangular pennant and said: 'That's for your bicycle. All the boys in Eichkamp have pretty little pennants like that on their bikes.' Of course, like everything else, she didn't mean it politically at all. It was just uplifting and celebratory. In Potsdam the elderly Field Marshal and his young Chancellor had exchanged a historic handshake: Garrison Church, Hohenzollern, the old flags and standards of the Prussian regiments, it was all so pious, and afterwards, so rousing and uplifting, the song of the good comrade walking by your side – and then my mother went to Hermann Tietz, even though he was Jewish, and bought her first swastika pennant.*

The Nazis had an unerring sense for the effects of provincial theatre. They had everything that was needed to stage a Wagner opera in a suburb, with all the fake magic of Yggdrasil and the *Götterdämmerung*,* so that the same people who normally listened to *Frau Luna* or *Die Fledermaus* were gripped and transfigured. Intoxication and transfiguration are the keywords of fascism, for the side it presents to the world, just as terror and death are the keywords for the reverse, and I think the people of Eichkamp too enjoyed allowing themselves to be intoxicated and transfigured. That was their Achilles heel. It was where they were defenceless. Suddenly you were somebody. You were something better, something higher: a German. The German land was blessed.

So that autumn my mother began to read the new Reich Chancellor's book. Deep down she had always felt the urge towards something higher. It was in her blood. She came from an old Silesian family, somewhat scruffy and always in debt, which had slowly migrated from Bohemia to Prussia. My mother, like Hitler, was 'artistic' and 'somehow Catholic'. She was devoted to an indescribable form of private Catholicism: spiritual, yearning, confused. She raved about Rome and the Rhineland carnival, when she had mislaid her key she confidently prayed to St Anthony, and sometimes she hinted to us children that she was destined by birth for higher things: she could have been a sister in the Ursuline Order. We could never find out why this nervous and delicate woman, who could at times engage very seriously with anthroposophy and vegetarianism, had married this good-natured craftsman's son from Berlin-Stralau. He wasn't really her social equal, and he was also Protestant in that gruff Berlin way that is expressed even today in a rabid and scornful anti-Catholicism.

My father didn't get particularly far with school. As for so many German men at the time, the war had been a blessing. My father was not a militarist, he was a peaceful, even-tempered man, but war suddenly made everything so clear and simple. He seems to have been steady and brave, and by 1916 he had been wounded near Verdun; since then his somewhat modest career as an official had gone steadily upwards. First the godsend of the bullet to the head, then the Iron Cross, then NCO, then sergeant, and in the end he must have been something like a second lieutenant; at any rate, in 1918 he brought an officer's sword home from the war, and some kind of paper that entitled him to start a 'state career' all the way from the bottom. For a while he carried files, then later he pulled a trolley along the long corridors of the Prussian Ministry of Culture, and after that he became deputy assistant, assistant, office manager and finally even inspector.

That was not the end of my father's rise. By the time we moved to Eichkamp he was probably a senior inspector; he was now an official for life and able to afford a little house of his own, he drew a ministerial allowance and achieved the rank of senior civil servant under Chancellor Brüning. That was a summit as far as he was concerned, a breathtaking peak for which the state was owed lifelong loyalty and submission. For all his life he took the 8.23 to the Ministry, he travelled upholstered class, read the *Deutsche Allgemeine Zeitung* and the *Lokal-Anzeiger* at home, never joined the Party, never knew anything about Auschwitz. He never subscribed to the *Völkischer Beobachter*, which was too noisy and combative for him, but at 8.20, when he passed the newspaper kiosk at Eichkamp station, he would buy himself the *Völkischer Beobachter* and hold it in front of his nose for twenty minutes all the way to Friedrichstrasse station, so that everyone else could tell how loyal he was to the new, völkisch state.* He left the newspaper on his seat at Friedrichstrasse. At the Ministry he sometimes protested in very small circles against gross injustices by the new gentlemen in charge. Political jokes were also allowed; he particularly liked the ones that started with 'Hermann'.

For a lifetime he came home at 4.21, always on the same train, always in the same second-class compartment, if there was room, always by the same corner window, always with a briefcase full of work in his right hand; with his left he showed his monthly ticket in its bright metal wallet. He never jumped off the moving train. He had reached his destination, he was a German state official, and whether the name of the chancellor was Noske or Ebert, Scheidemann or Brüning, Papen or Hitler, he was always bound by a duty of loyalty and fidelity.* His office was his world and his heaven was his wife. And at the time his wife was reading *Mein Kampf*, was 'somehow Catholic' and only briefly 'political'.

I don't know what things were actually like before Hitler in all those poky little estate houses – I assume it wasn't very different from life in our own house. Getting up at half past six, washing, having breakfast and presenting a friendly face, going to school, coming home, food in the oven, then upstairs for homework, the open window, life was enticing, but then back to the schoolbooks, then my father coming home at around half past four, a tiny hope that something might happen, that he might have brought something unusual back

from town, but nothing ever happened in our house, everything was normal, regulated, orderly. Had it not been for my
mother's illnesses, those bizarre and fantastical illnesses of
a highly imaginative woman – my youth here in Eichkamp
would have been a single day that went on for fifteen years,
fifteen years of nothing, simply nothing that might have been
considered peaks or troughs, fears or joys: fifteen years of
the compulsion, the murderous compulsive neurosis, of an
obedient German civil servant.

Sundays, of course, were the worst. We had to sleep late,
because it was Sunday, after all. Sunday in 1931 in Eichkamp: breakfast was infinitely protracted, the solemn, fixed
expressions of my parents, because it was Sunday, after all.
Monosyllabic exchanges about the eggs, which were always
held to be too hard or too soft. Attempts to be friendly
towards one another in that Sunday way, attempts to talk
about the weather, misunderstandings, the first beginnings
of an argument, then silence again. Into the silence, the
pointless and slightly malicious question of whether anyone
wanted a top-up of coffee. We wore our Sunday best, so of
course we had to be incredibly careful when pouring the
coffee.

Early on, I had got used to looking out of the window in
a stiff and persistent way in such situations. I would always
imagine that I was sitting not at the family table, but somewhere outside in the garden, having breakfast all by myself
in a leafy glade, a glorious feast of solitude. It must have been
an angry and scornful way of ignoring the others. Even at
the age of thirteen I could stir my coffee cup with apparent
absent-mindedness and study a pine tree in the wind with
great interest while my parents made monosyllabic obser-
vations about the cream cake, the maid or the state of our
baroque dresser. But this pointed absent-mindedness of

mine was not even noticed. Nothing at all was noticed in our house. We sat there like puppets that couldn't reach one another. We dangled from wires held somewhere far above.

After breakfast there were certain highlights. My father would start winding up our big grandfather clock, which stood in our dining room like a long, upright coffin. The carved oak front would be unbolted and the big glass door solemnly opened, the massive, heavy brass key fished from the display cabinet. Then with a resolute grip of his hand my father suddenly held the huge pendulum. The ticking in our dining room stopped. Then there would be an oppressive silence, followed by the turning and creaking of the clock-work mechanism, and the springs would rise in short, tight jerks. Dust swirled up. The procedure had to be performed twice, and then of course the striking mechanism with its bongs had to be tightened once again, after which my father's strength had magically passed into the workings of the clock. It would now go on ticking and bonging for another week, the week could begin, Sunday was safe, the case was closed. At last my father would light a twenty-pfennig cigar from Boenicke.

After that there would be regular discussions about churchgoing. For some incomprehensible reason the fixed rule in our house was that one of us had to go to church every Sunday. We weren't at all churchy or pious – but still. My father stayed out of the discussion since he was Protestant and Protestants in Berlin don't go to church. My mother always had a powerful need for spiritual consolation and the company of higher powers – and had done since long before Hitler. She promised herself comfort and strength from this, and probably felt reminded of her time in the convent, but unfortunately the compromised state of her health meant that she was only rarely able to attend. Like almost all women she had a delicate heart condition and particularly on a Sunday, when she began to straighten the fur jacket that she now owned, it was very likely that she would suffer one of those sudden, unexpected heart tremors. When that happened the medicinal drops would have to be fetched, and she would lie flat on the sofa. Consequently the task of going to church usually fell to me. It was simply that it was passed to the weakest of us. I was twelve, I wasn't Catholic at all, I wasn't Protestant either, I was simply nothing, like almost everyone in Eichkamp at the time. I was the youngest, I couldn't defend myself and so I was sent to church on behalf of the whole family, like the scapegoat among the Jews.

Yes, that's pretty much how things were in Eichkamp back in the days before Hitler. At lunchtime the whole place would smell of Sauerbraten or calf's head, with spinach or kohlrabi from the garden.* I was always supposed to tell the rest of the family what the priest had said in church. I could never remember exactly, and appeared obstinate. Then my mother would start nervously fiddling with her knife and fork, she would poke them into the potatoes as if they were chopsticks, as if by resorting to ritualistic eating gestures she could somehow avert the guilt of my meagre faith. Sometimes, as he placed his napkin over his belly, my father would make one last scornful remark about Catholicism. That would make my mother sit bolt upright. There were arguments. While all this was going on there would be requests for gravy and potatoes and I would gaze fascinatedly out of the window once again.

Then, at three, off we went to the cinema. It was a children's screening: tickets were thirty pfennigs. I usually didn't want to go, but at that time on Sunday I always had to go to the Rivoli in Halensee with my sister. Again there would be those empty, pointless walks through Eichkamp, again we would walk side by side like puppets, as if we were being pulled upwards on wires. Before we got to Halensee we had to pass the railway repair workshops. The walk took us down a long, dark tunnel, past low, grey concrete walls, and down twisting passageways, then suddenly it was bright again: a long, miserable road, suburban silence, cobblestones, weeds and scraps of paper in the gutter – an unexpected proletarian world. This was where the railway workers lived: grey railwaymen's apartments, monotonous and washed out, Prussian barracks-style of 1880, weary faces by the windows. They were 'the Reds', as our parents had warned us. I didn't really know what that meant, but you could tell by looking at them that the Reds were dangerous. There must have been a reason why they eked out their wretched existences here, between Eichkamp and Halensee, in the no man's land of the Berlin suburbs, as if hidden behind prison walls. A red rabble lived here – 'rabble' being my parents' favourite term for everyone who was beneath us: craftsmen and maids, beggars and scissor-sharpeners, the people who rang our doorbells in the morning and of course really wanted to break in.

The Red rabble also lived on the eastern periphery of Eichkamp, just before the railway station. These were estate houses recently built by the Workers' Welfare Institution much to the chagrin of the old residents of Eichkamp. The small houses were just as grim and unornamented as ours, they were as alike as two peas in a pod, but my parents always insisted that they were quite different: poor, cheap and mass-produced and far removed from the sedate style of the long-term inhabitants. Indeed, the Reds lived differently here. Their houses were set right at the back of the long, narrow strips of garden, as if an attempt were being made to hide them. Stone paths lined with flowers led rather shakily to the front door, and outside the houses chickens could be seen pecking about, and women wearing washed-out aprons and with bright blue scarfs on their heads, carrying wooden tubs and zinc buckets and working and toiling like German artisans. It was a strange, alien world that I had never entered, and which filled me with a mixture of curiosity and contempt. For nine years I had walked past the fences of the Reds carrying my schoolbag – I was, after all, a grammar-school boy and would certainly be the first in our family to sit the grammar-school leaving exam, the Abitur. I only dared to look curiously from a distance; this was a remote, forbidden, low world, there was hope and fear of what lay below – the Reds had broken into Eichkamp.

Our Eichkamp was something more elevated, more respectable. My mother never wore a blue headscarf, she didn't carry tubs back and forth, but she was often elaborately ill, she always described herself as 'suffering', and that allowed her to look superior. I never found out what her ailment actually was. That's why she often kept a maid. The maids always smelled of sweat, they cost thirty marks a month, had fat, spongy upper arms and were usually dismissed after four or five months, 'at the drop of a hat', as my parents put it. They always had a baby, and as a little boy I initially associated this with the smell of sweat. I only heard later that 'this rabble' were unspeakably dirty and libidinous, that they were notorious for consorting with soldiers on their Sunday evenings off, and as a kind of divine punishment for that behaviour they would have a baby nine months later.

No one at home talked about where babies came from. My parents were not only apolitical, they were unerotic and asexual too. Perhaps all of these things belonged together, and love was no more a topic of conversation than politics. It was held to be too low. Sexuality in particular must have been incredibly low and indelicate, because when I finally turned sixteen and, like all the boys in Eichkamp, had been masturbating for a long time, I once received a lengthy piece of advice from my parents, who must have noticed something. Yes, they had noticed something.

One evening there was a long, thin leaflet on my bedside table. I was very surprised, because my dealings with my parents had not previously involved printed material. I immediately understood that something extraordinary must be happening. I started reading. It was a mild, gentle, kindly educational text that began with grasses and bumble-bees, then spoke of the sun, then spoke of the miracles of the power of God, finally turned its attention to the strength of man, and to the terrible deadly sins of weakness. It was said to weaken the spine. But I still didn't quite understand the connection, it was all a bit too pious for me in those days. It was a Catholic educational leaflet that my mother had, in her desperation, acquired from the Ursulines. She never mentioned it, I never mentioned it. We never brought the subject up at home, and had I not felt things stirring within my own body, I might still have believed in our maids' fertile sweat by the time I was twenty. That was how things were in our family. The lower-middle-class German house excludes from its own cramped rooms not only the state but also love. We might wonder – purely sociologically – what is left of life, without politics and sexuality.

In our house, what was left were our neighbours, for example. There were certain relationships, tentative attempts, efforts to reach out to our fellows, demarcations, attempts to break out. Sometimes when I came home from the Rivoli with my sister at about half past five on Sunday afternoon, the Marburgers would be sitting there. They were the neighbours from across the road. They were stiff, refined people, whose childlessness contributed strangely to their elegance.

She was quite tall, he quite short, they both wore their Sunday best, which always smelled slightly of mothballs, they sat stiffly upright on tall chairs, stirring their coffee with silver spoons and occasionally making sharp remarks about the neighbours. They always made me shiver.

Herr Marburger was also a senior civil servant. He too had worked his way up from the bottom, which put him unambiguously on a par with my father, but since Herr Marburger was only a senior civil servant in the Ministry of Agriculture, my mother always felt somewhat superior to the Marburgers. My father could never quite understand that. Sometimes in the evening, when the Marburgers had left, they had long debates about the matter in which my mother violently insisted that there was a difference between only administering cows and forests as Herr Marburger did, or, like my father, art. In fact, my father now worked in the administration of the Music College on Hardenbergstrasse, which allowed his wife, who might once have become a singer in the convent, to inform him that our involvement with art gave us a quite different rank. That was how fine the distinctions were in Eichkamp.

Sometimes the Stefans also paid us a visit. Herr Stefan was admittedly only a senior inspector, and at the post office for that. But his eldest son, Oskar, was already studying medicine. That in turn gave the Stefans a strange and insidious kind of superiority, which they were maliciously able to play up with occasional references to university and the daunting morals of student fraternities. That wrong-footed my parents, leaving them temporarily helpless and also giving them a sense of oppressive inferiority.

It was now 1931. There were more than four million unemployed in the country, the global economic crisis was shaking the planet, in Berlin the Communists and the

Brownshirts were engaging in bloody street battles, one day the banks were closed and in between, from the Roman Café to the Ullstein publishing house, the hectic twenties were played out, with Expressionism and Russian film triumphant in Berlin. But my parents were aware of none of that, they registered only these finest of distinctions within Eichkamp society and made it clear to me why I could consort with the Naumanns' children but not with the Lehmanns'. For the Lehmanns were in fact proper academics with the title 'Dr' emblazoned on their nameplate at the garden fence, and that was too high up for us. My parents had a clear sense of up and down. You had to feel it. The people down below were a rabble and the people above were out of reach.

The Ernst family, living opposite and to the left, were unattainably high as well: he was a doctor, which gave them several different kinds of superiority. My parents felt honoured when they said hello to them, they respected Herr Ernst's imposing face, which was decorated with a number of fencing scars, they observed, not without some admiration, their extravagant lifestyle, which was distinctly different from ours in that they had occasional taxi journeys and their garden was lit up in the evening. And when one day we saw that they even had a car, a little black Opel P4, that was – long before Hitler – a small revolution in Eichkamp. My parents watched enviously from behind the curtains as the Ernst family climbed aboard this strange vehicle on Sunday afternoons and trundled away as if summoned by higher powers. Those were clear signs of their having been chosen.

And many of the residents of Eichkamp were like my parents in those days: those Nissens and Wessels, Naumanns and Neumanns, those Stefans and Schuhmanns, Lehmanns and Strübings. They had all come from lowly backgrounds and their achievements were modest; they always lived in fear of slipping back down again, they wanted to stay up, they were somebody now and had that infallible sense of rank in its very finest distinctions. They were apolitical and unerotic, they read the *Lokal-Anzeiger*, they solved crosswords on Sunday evening, they unfailingly voted for the German National People's Party, sprinkled the lawn and swore by order and convention.* The Blankenburgers backed on to the rear of our garden. For a while I was friends with their son Friedrich. Herr Blankenburger was a senior teacher, and one day I wasn't allowed to go to his house any more either. My parents forbade it. It was not because of the academic side of things. It was worse than that. The Marburgers had casually mentioned on one of their Sunday visits that Herr Blankenburger was a Red – him too. He was a member of the Social Democrats. The older residents of Eichkamp were outraged. That was in the summer of 1932.

So Hitler's Reich actually descended on Eichkamp like a divine force. No one had called for it, no one had fought against it. It simply arrived, as a season comes. The time was ripe. Everything here was nature, nothing was society. No one had been part of it, no one had been a Nazi. It came from far-away Berlin and now hung like a cloud over Eichkamp: at a high altitude, and with beautiful plumage. In our house it had little to do with patriotic motives. I had barely heard a thing about Germany's defeat in 1918 and the shame of Versailles in my parents' conversations. The German disgrace was never felt in Eichkamp; it was probably more at home in Potsdam. The negative aspects of German history were seldom mentioned in Eichkamp. There was only ever the fear of slipping back down the ladder again, yet now here was someone who wanted to carry them higher and higher as if borne aloft on wings. That's what it was. It was simply too beautiful.

Now everything became so broad and high and hopeful. The First of May, which had always been perplexing to my parents because of its association with the Reds, now became a friendly day of celebration in Eichkamp too, and with its many flags and songs it recalled the *Mastersingers of Nuremberg*. In November the artists of the Staatsoper appeared on Unter den Linden collecting for the Winter Relief Fund; singers and actors trooped down the street rattling red collecting tins. My mother cooked the first stew of the year with a hint of commiseration, and that Sunday we ate that lumpy barley broth with a feeling of having done something for the Volksgemeinschaft.* That was something quite new in Eichkamp – the national community. Then the block warden came and collected our two marks fifty, and we were given a badge. That was new too. A benign baritone sang on the radio, I think his name was Willy Schneider and he still sings the same things today: 'Why is it so lovely by the Rhine?' and 'Drink a little glass of wine'. That was the new age we were living in: a bit of grandeur and cosiness. There was a lot of singing in Germany at the time. Young people wore such trim uniforms, Labour Service was held to be a good thing, the shouldered shovels made sense to the people of Eichkamp, and now there were so many holidays with massive marches and announcements. A procession of greatness passed through our lives around this time.

Hitler's invasion of our house – number 35 Im Eichkamp – was essentially an aesthetic event. It was all about beauty. The man was an artist, after all, a master-builder and a painter, and in his youth in Vienna he had 'inwardly struggled through', as my mother put it. She was sympathetic to that – admittedly she was thinking more in moral than political terms, since she herself had once wanted to be an artist. And now he was building opera houses and art museums all over the place, he was tearing down half of Berlin, planning everything on a large scale, creating magnificent new ministries, a Reich Chancellery that had the outward appearance of a Greek temple, he was designing clean roads all across the country: it gave my mother a physical sense of well-being. It was now that she joined the Nazi Cultural Community; that meant you could see *Die Fledermaus* at reduced prices and hear Elly Ney and see Emmy Sonnemann, who had by now made it too, standing by the side of her powerful husband.* All the Germans were making it now. And the music, the glorious German music, the art! Now it was being confirmed to us that art was worth more than agriculture, and a senior civil servant in the Ministry of Culture was higher up than one in the Ministry of Agriculture. The new age was 'musisch' – artistic; that was my mother's favourite word at the time.

I remember our first holiday in 1934. A hot July morning, we're sitting at the Schlesischer Bahnhof on the holiday train to Hirschberg. My mother in her fancy floral dress, surrounded by lots of suitcases and bags, and the food is being distributed around the compartment. Then my father comes in with a morning newspaper. A big bold headline. He reads. They talk to each other, they argue in serious tones, their faces embarrassed and anxious. There is talk of sexuality and something else before that, I don't understand it, and I hear that 'such people' should appear in front of a proper court instead of being shot in their beds.* My father was unhappy about the procedure. Those were the first clouds in our holiday sky. I remember the morning after 'Reichskristallnacht'. Tauentzienstrasse is scattered with broken glass, the Jewish shop windows have been smashed, and now Brownshirts with shoulder straps are standing next to them and observing the passers-by. People walk past in dejected silence. In the evening my father tells us that synagogues have been burned and the 'rabble' – here was that word again – had broken Jewish shop windows and looted Jewish homes. Anxious faces at home, silent outrage: did the Führer know about this? My mother had her private concerns about this man. She was Catholic, and the Concordat must have come as a source of deep satisfaction to her. But subsequently there were pastoral letters, which were read out from the pulpit and had a more reflective tone. There was so much about the monasteries and convents in the papers. Every day when searching for currency crimes the police discovered bad practices among the monks' habits, there was talk of pederasty, I still didn't quite understand it, but it alarmed my mother that the Franciscans that she loved so much, that they of all people could succumb to such a vice. Later different pastoral letters came which pledged serious and circumspect allegiance to the völkisch state, but which then went on to speak of cases of euthanasia, which were unacceptable.* It was a difficult situation for my mother: on the one hand she fervently respected the clergy, on the other hand she was so attracted by the artistic side – 'das Musische' – of the new Reich. It was the old conflict between the ethical and the aesthetic: Kierkegaard had arrived in Eichkamp.

But such reflective moments could not conceal the fact that we were living in a great new age. The Reich and the youth, art and the state – only now did the people of Eichkamp see what kind of forces they were. Everything was so solemn now: before the Führer's speeches, Beethoven concerts on the radio; the great man also went quite modestly to Bayreuth; and nude statues of young men were saluting from outside post offices with blazing torches in their hands – a Hellenic springtime for Germany. Admittedly no one from Eichkamp had ever been to Greece. The construction of the massive stadium for the 1936 Olympic Games was under way on Heerstrasse, and even Eichkamp was bathed in reflected glory. The biggest assembly hall in the world was being built right beside the railway station, its huge ceiling entirely without supporting columns, and our sleepy little station was now called 'Deutschlandhalle' and had an exit to the rear only for visitors to the hall. That lifted us a little more.

In fact, so much grandeur stood in a strange, bizarre contrast with our little estate, but when I come to think about it, that was where the fascination really lay. The people of Eichkamp weren't used to things happening on this scale. It left them defenceless, and prone to a belief in miracles. They were like children, they were simply delighted to hear how wonderful it was to be a German, to see Germany becoming ever greater. And now the Reich was growing daily. Everything was improving by the day, everything was becoming ever more elevated, and since the people of Eichkamp were actually lower on the scale, they were happy to be carried a little higher by this upward surge. We kept rising further and further. Why not? Herr Berger said: 'At last it's our turn to enter world history – as is only fair.' Herr Stefan said: 'Now we're building motorways so that our postal service gets even faster.' Frau Marburger said: 'We'll adopt a child, now that so many German mothers are having children.' Herr Schumann said: 'And we're getting our colonies back too – that much is clear,' and brought his old sou'wester down from the loft. And Herr Nissen even placed his hopes on the Kaiser: 'The Hohenzollerns are on the way, someone's paid a visit to Doorn. You'll see!'*

One day, just after the Austrian Anschluss, I met Frau Stefan in the street.* I was just coming back from school. She said: 'What, you don't think our Führer was sent by God?' I had no idea that Frau Stefan was so pious, or that she believed in God. Her husband was only a postal inspector, after all. But this was possibly another thing that Hitler had brought to Eichkamp: the knowledge that there were such things as providence, eternal justice and an almighty God. Even in Eichkamp people were now talking a lot about these invisible powers. These were pious times. My mother had also copied out one of the Führer's phrases, for which she felt a conflicted admiration. She was keen to discuss the matter with me. He had said: 'By opposing the Jews I am doing the work of the Lord!' That was more or less what they were also saying in church – wasn't it? She always wanted to talk about this sentence, first with the clergy and later with me. She tried to understand anti-Semitism on a higher, theological level. You could say that everything at this time – autumn 1938 – was played out at a higher level in our house. Both Hitler and Eichkamp were quite high up at the time. A mood of piety had descended over the country.

Yes, if I remember correctly, that's more or less how things were in our house at this time. I know it's ugly to dig up such memories today. It's a little bit odd and embarrassing, and no one wants to admit that they joined in with it all in such a fervent and childish way. Today our country is swarming with resistance fighters, people on secret missions, internal emigrants and sly foxes who only appeared to conform so as to prevent worse things from happening. The Germans, a people of resistance fighters; the Germans, a people of persecuted victims. Oh, if only the SS and the Gestapo hadn't been around in those days, the people would have risen up against Hitler. They just weren't able to.

These are the new myths of our time, the benign prevalent lies of our historians, who all so conveniently acquit us, a patching-up of history that makes everything so intelligible – they explain the Nazi terror over Germany, apart from one thing: why the Germans loved this man, why they honestly cheered him, why they were willing to die for him in their millions. Look at military cemeteries all over the world: those buried there weren't, as in East Germany, uniformed men behind whom more uniformed men stood with their guns shouldered. They were honest believers, intoxicated enthusiasts, practically urging one another on to a hero's death. The only thing they were afraid of was turning up late for all those victories. And if someone in 1938 had dared to fire the fatal shot at Hitler, it wouldn't have taken an SS man or a Gestapo officer to catch him. The people themselves would have executed him for murdering the Messiah. That's how it was.

And yet – they weren't Nazis. The real Nazis had in fact come out of nowhere, they were five per cent of the population at most, they had never studied, they had no skills, they were human wrecks and would have gone to the wall after three or four months – had not all those good, decent Germans in Eichkamp put all their energy, their hard work, their faith and their fate into blindly supporting them. They had slipped so slowly from their petit-bourgeois dreams into this age of greatness, they now felt very much at ease, they were delighted by what this man had made of them. They never understood that it was they, all of them collectively, who had made this man. Without them he would never have emerged from the back room of the Hofbräuhaus.* Right until the end they always thought they owed everything to Hitler: the time of greatness and the time of dying.

My parents too believed that until the very end. October 1944. It was the business with the olive oil from Italy, a domestic quirk of fate that coincided more or less by chance with the disaster of history. I was coming back from the front; I hadn't seen my parents for four years. They had aged terribly; for four years of the war in Eichkamp they had lived only on food stamps and now their faces were exhausted, 'rationised', as people said at the time. They looked like addicts suddenly deprived of morphine: shivering and thin. My mother, who had dyed her hair a lovely shade of black during the years of greatness, had now become snow-white and truly pious – even then I sensed that after Hitler there would be a massive upsurge in churchgoing in our country. There was so much disappointed trustfulness there. And my father, who had never understood those peaks in religious faith, now understood nothing any more, he was helpless, he just kept shaking his head, his neck sticking curiously dry and leathery out of the collar that was now too wide for him, and he just kept quietly complaining: 'That crowd, those criminals, what have they done to us! After the war we'll all be dragged to Russia, that much is clear.' He didn't actually have anything to reproach himself with. He had never joined the Party. He would get a glowing report: white as snow.

Eichkamp commuter station, 30 October 1944. The Russians are in Silesia, the Americans in the Ardennes. My leave is over. They walk me to the train. The cold, deserted platform is draughty. They stand there in their black coats, which sag around their thin bodies. There is weakness, hunger, fear in their faces. Some form of love darts aimlessly from their eyes. Weariness among the wrinkles, a dying lower-middle class lying to itself once again. Family discussions – we've still got *you*, embarrassed laughter, worried advice from my mother about how I should behave at the front: Always dress warmly, never stick your neck out, only ever do what everyone else is doing. Reassurances that we will soon see each other happily again. The train pulls in. I pick up my luggage. I'm twenty-five, she's nearly sixty. I feel strong, they look like old people in their quivering helplessness. A familiar, awkward hug. I board the commuter train and close the door. I go to the window and lean out.

There they are, standing out there, the ones who brought you into the world: Eichkamp parents. They look a little comical in their helplessness, it could almost make one laugh, but I feel more like crying. Now they're waving their handkerchiefs, they're getting smaller and smaller, they look almost like Philemon and Baucis.* I know I'll never see them again. Never. This is the end, their death. The Russians will come and their son is away. But you're our only one. We still have *you*. You're the last thing we have. My God, they've stripped us of everything. You're our hope – that's what they cling to. Another illusion, they've always lived on illusions.

This is how it will be: they will fall ill, they will lie alone somewhere, with the Russians all around, they will die alone somewhere. The funeral will be pitiful. There are so many dead people here in Berlin now. Suicide is going around. There are hardly any coffins left. Even that kind of wood is running low. They'll put you in bags, that's right, in bags like vegetables, that's what your Hitler has done for you. And dump you in a hole somewhere near the Wannsee.

But for now they're still there. They're tiny black dots by now that still cling to me, reluctant to let go – my parents. They don't stop waving: You're not going to leave us, are you?

I'm long out of sight. Throat tight, I hurl myself down on the polished yellow wooden bench, and my gas-mask container makes a loud crash. I think: Thank God that's over. You'll never see them again. That's behind you now. You'll never go back to Eichkamp – never again.

A REQUIEM FOR URSULA

'Ve been on the suburban train for a long time. It's almost a forty-five-minute journey from Eichkamp to Priesterweg. After that the train empties. The city dissolves. The air is damp and hazy. Signals stand wetly in the fog. Forgotten names from my childhood fly past the window: Gesundbrunnen, Papestrasse, Lichtenrade, Gleisdreieck, Mariendorf – unexplored territories, both then and now. Berlin is very eastern. The people in Berlin are called Labude and Kabuschke and were born in the Spreewald, in the Lausitz, in Silesia. I've only noticed that since I've been coming from the West. They have pale, weary faces with Wendish cheekbones and thin, colourless lips. And when they sit opposite you here in the suburban train, in trousers that are slightly too baggy, coats that are slightly too long, and some women with scarves around their heads, and when it's already getting dark again at three – who's going to tell me in the gloom just beyond Papestrasse that I'm not travelling towards Katowice, not towards Poznań, not towards Vilnius? Berlin is very eastern.

No one gets out at Priesterweg station. Mechanical movements. The platform is high and narrow and draughty, and everything made of iron looks rusty. There is a smell of November. An open view of damp fields: allotment summer houses with felt roofs, beer bottles left over from the summer, spades, tins and reddish-brown flowerpots. A water tower stands as imperiously as a concrete mushroom among the gardens, then comes a coal merchant's depot. Stairs, passageways, tunnels – why are railway underpasses in Berlin always so bare, so high-ceilinged and so draughty? I hear my footsteps echoing off the walls. Somewhere a locomotive whistles, and signals fall over my head. A small van rattles past on three wheels, carrying old-fashioned furniture which might belong to a pensioner who's decided to move to Südende. And then, as always just before cemeteries, there are those nurseries with flowers for the dead and iron wreaths leaning against the fence: kiosks of a pious transience. 'All kinds of funeral decorations', I read. Then come the stonemasons' workshops, where massive palm fronds are carved in marble and blank headstones stand waiting for names. Sometimes there's a shop selling coffins too: carved wood, polished brown and wide open in the window, inviting to a lavish end.

I avoided coming here for a long time. I should have come years ago. It's a long way from Frankfurt to Südende. People coming to Berlin make straight for Zoo, make straight for the Hansaviertel and the Messedamm – they always avoid the cemeteries. I haven't been here for three years. There are feelings of worry and a guilty conscience inside me. Some duties are indispensable. Even those who couldn't find their way to one another in life, in death they are strangely connected. They say: Graves admonish. But perhaps it's only that graves are as tough as scars, they stir up ancient stories. Like old people, they always tell the same story over and over again: monotonous, boring, accusatory; no one wants to hear it. The language of graves is like the language of pensioners: That's how it was, it will never be like that again, life is over.

The last one remaining has to learn this language. Everything always rests on the last one; the whole burden of memory rests on him. I carry within me the burden of five people who once lived. I barely knew them, but now they live in me and will only die with me. That's called family, Eichkamp family, and it happened a long time ago. It all flows together in me, and if I were a decent human being I would move to Berlin permanently so that I could regularly stand by their graves on the Day of Penance, on the Day of the Commemoration of the Dead, on Good Friday and so on. The last one is always something like a cemetery administrator. His life is nothing but memory and pious preservation. I don't like that, I don't want that. When I come to Berlin, I'm still looking for life. I stroll to Zoo and to Hardenbergstrasse, I travel to Moabit and smell the smells of Spandau and Halensee, I notice the fine distinctions between Schöneberg and Charlottenburg. And everywhere I go I still expect something wonderful. So for three years I haven't been here, here at St Matthew's cemetery in Südende.

A red-brick building from the 1880s, the severity of the Wilhelmine age, Prussian air in the passageways, cardboard panels on the walls: cemetery rules, visiting times, rulings of the magistrate and the parish – the church, a communal institute of burial. A short, thin little man sits behind a wooden barrier flicking through heavy ledgers. He is flicking through the annals of the dead as if they were alive, secret troops under his command, who are out there in the field, as real to him as troops in an orderly room. And I say: 'Yes, her name was Ursula K. She was buried here in 1938, early April. I visited her here often. She was my sister.' The cemetery administrator makes a great effort. As always in Prussia everything here is recorded and ordered, and in fact it should only take a few turned pages to find every dead person straight away. I just wanted to know her plot number because it's so easy to get lost among the graves. The dead are very similar to one another, and there is nothing more dreadful than to end up mourning by the wrong grave. But the process seems to be difficult. 'Thirty-eight?' the old man asks. 'April thirty-eight?' And he starts taking down new ledgers from the shelf, wets his index finger with a green sponge and goes on flicking through his yellowing forest of the dead.

The room is full of crackling sounds. The yellow paper crackles like parchment being wrapped around something, and the crackling of a fire can be heard from the little iron stove. It's warm in the room, overheated in that eastern way; in Berlin they always take heating seriously, I think, just as they do in Vilnius and Leningrad; they are furiously deter- mined to keep winter at bay, and I start to unbutton my coat and jacket. 'I'm off,' I say, 'I'll find it – I've been here many times.' But the little administrator has got his teeth into it now, he senses a case that needs to be dealt with, he has assumed a serious fiscal task, and if something is not in his files, how could it be out there in the field? It goes on like that for a good quarter of an hour, every imaginable register and file is examined, thick tomes from the pre-war years are consulted. Something grotesque seems to have happened, a corpse administered by the Prussian state has gone missing – an unthinkable event in Berlin. Then the old man suddenly looks at me brightly, taps himself triumphantly on the fore- head and asks in a flash: 'April thirty-eight, you say, Ursula K., you say? Of course,' he says. 'The row of graves in Section S,' picks up another big ledger, flicks curiously through the register of the dead, looks through the list of names, and then suddenly his whole face lights up. The joys of administration. 'We've got it!' he shouts, leaps up from the office stool and eagerly drags everything over to me. He is delighted and, run- ning his pencil down the list, says triumphantly: 'It's not there any more, it's gone, I mean the grave. We levelled it last year!'

And I learn to my amazement that graves can die like people, that it can happen to you: you come home and your wife is dead, and equally you can visit a grave years later and find that the grave is gone, the grave itself has died and there is nothing left, nothing at all. I learn to my horror that the twenty-five-year lease ran out two years ago. For more than a year a piece of paper would have hung out there in the corridor, for more than a year they would have been trying to warn relatives who couldn't be reached otherwise that they needed to renew the lease or else the plot would be cleared and another body put inside. Ground is in short supply. And no one visited throughout that whole year, no one wanted to renew the grave, so that January – 'Wait,' the old man says, 'I can tell you exactly, if you're interested: there's a Franziska Busch there now, where your estimable sister lay.'

My estimable sister – for a moment I feel stiff and anxious, guilt wells up, a paralysing fear of the void that now exists: she's gone, it's impossible, it can't be. I always went to Zoo and Hardenbergstrasse, I sat in the Schillertheater and dined at the Kampinsky, while they were hunting for me here. Simply levelled, just like that, simply put something else on top of it, who'd have thought such things are allowed: they can't just take our dead away from us. Now all of a sudden she no longer exists, I'm told, my sister has been erased from the world and, strictly speaking, I'm the one who killed her. So that's what guilt is like, now you're feeling it for the first time. I have destroyed her grave; it's an ancient taboo, of course, like incest or matricide. Ancient guilt is now being awakened. Nothing remains of her – now she lives only in me. Everything comes together inside me. The last one remaining always bears the whole burden of memory. If I cease to remember now, she will be dead for ever. So I will have to remember.

*

Austria had returned to the Reich. There was much Greater-German cheering in the air at Eichkamp, much gratitude towards Vienna. The world-spirit was passing through our country, history was happening right outside our door: our front door was painted green, it was made of pinewood, and it had just been given its first security lock with chain – to keep out burglars.

It was March 1938. Germany was in good shape, but we were not like those who push their way to the front at such times. Those people are always the same and, as we know, they are not always the best. Noise didn't suit us. In the end, in many middle-class houses the Greater-German cheering turned into contemplation, in Eichkamp Greater-German shouting passed quietly into loyalty. We would have been something like a respectable German family at the time, one of many millions who participated gratefully and industriously in the sudden rise of our people.

The evening had passed as Sunday evenings always did in our house. We had had dinner: sausage sandwiches, cheese and bread, and beer, two tall and narrow bottles of Schultheiss-Patzenhofer. We had listened to the radio, flicked through the entertainment supplement of the *Lokal-Anzeiger*, come across a crossword. There was always a tributary of the river Werra or the hero of a Wagner opera, five letters ending in T, needing to be looked up. My mother liked to embroider something flowery. My father flicked through files and filled the air around his head with clouds of blue smoke. At around nine o'clock my mother, supplied with a few books and medications, retreated upstairs to the bedroom. She had recently taken to reading: she read Coué and Brauchle, she read Steiner and Chaplain Fahsel and engaged very seriously with the advantages of vegetarianism.* It was rumoured at the time that even the great man in the Reich

Chancellery could not perform his wonders without abstaining from meat. The genius was a vegetarian. Here mysterious connections seemed to exist. My mother always wanted to explore them.

At ten o'clock my father would listen to the news. There were reports from all over the world, there were congratulations, best wishes and many declarations of loyalty – not only from within Germany. Then, at ten past ten, it was my father's turn to go to bed. I had been in my room for a while, lying in bed, hearing him shuffle along the corridor and going downstairs to the basement, where the water and gas had to be turned off. My mother always insisted that the main gas pipe in the basement needed to be firmly bolted shut and the spanner to be left on her bedside table. The big, slightly rusty square spanner lay right beside Chaplain Fahsel's sermons, and together they gave us a strange feeling of security. I heard my father coming up the stairs, heard him locking the bedroom door twice from inside, heard my parents' monosyllabic conversations, heard my father opening the wardrobe and dropping his high boots on the floor, and heard the bed creaking. I lay next to my brightly embroidered wall hanging, a fake Persian carpet from the Wertheim department store that roused me to wonderful flights of fancy. I always tried to pursue the intricate mazes, the twisting paths between red and black, to solve the mysteries of the Orient. In the midst of that I fell asleep. Dreamlike figures came chasing after me. Now Eichkamp began to sleep and its breathing deepened. The whole of Eichkamp dreamed its way deeply and peacefully into Germany's future.

The next morning I was awoken by screams. I heard blows, splintering pine wood; it was half-past eight according to my alarm clock. Everyone was in a state of wild excitement, horrified, as if an official had incomprehensibly overslept by half an hour. I dashed to the corridor in my pyjamas, with bare feet that my father always forbade lest I catch a cold, but nobody cared about that right now. Her door had been smashed in, and the lock and some shattered wood were still attached to the frame; the wood was fibrous and yellow, and the door was dangling at a strange angle on its hinges. Her window was wide open, outside there was a mild spring light, and there lay Ursula in bed – I felt as if I was seeing her for the first time. She lay stiff and white on the pillows, her hands were folded as if in prayer, her brown hair fell softly over the pillow, she lay there as lovely and graceful as a department-store Madonna, and from the left corner of her mouth a dark red trickle, almost black, ran diagonally over her white skin to the pillow, where it formed a big bloody stain on the fresh linen.

I felt as if I knew all this already. It was almost like a Puccini opera, act four, Mimi's death: my God, how many times we had seen that in the Deutsche Oper under Artur Rother, under Leopold Ludwig, under Schmid-Isserstedt. Red dance shoes had been thrown around, and a white ballgown was draped over a chair, and various items of underwear, delicate and pink, lay scattered girlishly over the floor, and beside a piece of linen lay a yellow glass tube which I picked up and which startled me. The inscription was flanked by two large death's heads on the left and right, the like of which I had only ever seen on SS caps. One skull stared at you menacingly with black eye sockets, and behind it two leg bones were crossed, and next to it, with two exclamation marks, were the words: 'Danger, poison!!' and I read the word 'sublimate', which meant nothing to me.

Ursula wasn't dead. She was crying. A quiet, suppressed whimpering issued from her lips, pressed close together, and when she tried to open her mouth, black blood shot out and formed a thick clot on the white pillow. She immediately closed her mouth again.

I stood there and felt a strange sensation of peace and acceptance; I could see with clarity. I was nineteen, I was preparing for my Abitur, I knew, like all nineteen-year-olds, much more than my parents, I had heard some things about Homer and Socrates, I had learned of the high deeds of the Teutons and Tacitus' hymn of praise, and all of that now gave me a surprising superiority in terms of understanding. I understood the situation in a flash and thought: Of course, that happens. Why shouldn't one kill oneself? Such things are always in the air. I understand you, you don't need to say a word to me, just close your mouth firmly otherwise the blood will come, and then it will be like a Puccini opera. Please don't start up those self-pitying arias, I can't bear them, Mother intoned them so often at the piano in the study: Act four of Verdi's *Otello*, Act four of *La Traviata*, the final duet from *Aida*: 'Now the vault is firmly sealed.' We know about this in our house. Here you always die in Act four, it's demanded by our Eichkamp dramaturgy. No one spoke an intelligible word. My mother screamed from time to time and uttered shrill despairing sounds, and my father ran helplessly and agitatedly around the tiny room and explained categorically that my sister had done this to him and him alone. I am sure he had never read Freud, he didn't know what the Oedipus complex was, he had never heard of Electra either and still he referred the matter very directly to himself. There was a kind of primal terror and primal memory in us, a strange moment of truth amidst the rapture over the return of Austria, and I thought: You're lying there like a department-store Madonna, but you're like a man, you've shown courage. I envy you, Ursula, you have walked away from this German opera that we have seen so many times in Charlottenburg under Artur Rother. The props from Act four lie wildly scattered around, the character actors are now singing the requisite arias of horror, and the chorus is about to deliver the moral: that's how it is, that's the world, that was her life, so it is written everywhere. The last one remaining must slowly learn this language.

Suddenly there was something like love inside me. The fact that you did that brings me closer to you. You were my sister, there is no denying it, but did we ever notice? Kinship is a curious thing. The blood inside us remains always within us and cannot bind us together. Only when it spills from us, Ursula, only then does it bind us. Your blood is my blood, in this second you become my sister. We only ever walked side by side, to the Rivoli, to Zoo, to the Grunewald, to the Deutsche Oper. I didn't know what was going on inside you. And what did you know about me? We walked side by side like puppets held on high strings, we didn't know each other – how is family supposed to know each other? Family is cold-ness, strangeness, ice, no one can reach anyone else. Family words are formulas and family conversations frozen mis-understandings: yes and no and please and thank you and what do you want, what did you say, yes please, I'm coming, give me that, what's up, get a move on, wait a second, we're there, and how might things be at home? We exchanged these domestic formulas often, and still we were deaf to each other. Only now do I understand you. You are my sister. We are strangely united in death.

That Monday morning in March 1938 brought a wonderful and, we might say, musical vividness to our house; never did I feel as much at home in Eichkamp as I did when Ursula died. A dam had broken, a wall collapsed, and all of a sudden life returned to us: glorious, wild life, wonderful unease, and nothing worked any more. Chaos rose to the top. At our house everything had always worked all by itself, everything operated like clockwork: sleeping, waking, getting up, breakfast, the schoolbag and the walk to Eichkamp station – I always had my yellow monthly ticket in my pocket. That's how it had been my entire life. I had always longed for something extraordinary and wonderful: a summer day at the Teufelssee and lots of naked men and so much sadness in me – it must have been life I was looking for, and now all of a sudden it was there. Its name was chaos.

My parents couldn't cope with such a blow of fate. They ran desperately and helplessly around, they panted up the stairs and came back down, muttering something incomprehensible, they tore the windows open and closed them, they pulled the curtains shut and then threw them open again. My mother would sometimes collapse from exhaustion and fall into her club chair. She wailed loudly and then began to weep quietly, and later the weeping turned into prayer. From the study a pleading Our Father could be heard, followed by a higher and quicker Hail Mary. Meanwhile my father, who had never managed to commune on this higher level, had to look for the bunch of keys he had mislaid in all the excitement. And of course they were both confronted by a mystery, much worse and more incomprehensible than what happened seven years later when fate struck once more: in March again, March 1945, when British bombers left our house in ruins for ever – it must have been something like a foreshock within the closest circle of the family, an intimate vibration of world history. When things had a political nature, they almost made sense. In the closest circle they were incomprehensible. Family is mysterious.

My parents lamented their fate, which had taken such a disastrous turn. They spoke of the bosom of the family and children's ingratitude, and they listed their good deeds in the First World War, during inflation, throughout the Great Depression. There had always been milk, even in 1923, and all the schoolbooks they had bought, and all the money for summer camp and the whole burden of our education, everything had always gone well, everything was going well now – and then this by way of thanks: simply throwing life away as if it were nothing at all. They agreed that Ursula's desire not to go on living was an act of extraordinary ingratitude, a rejection of the order of God, my mother said, a rejection of the order of the state, my father said, and an act of sinful ingratitude towards them, and basically aimed only at them. Children owed their parents undying, lasting gratitude, and children who kill themselves are actually killing their parents, I learned, and I could see some truth in that last conclusion.

On that Monday morning my parents were really very lucky that they had me. In their despair they had left Ursula lying there all day, so intensely preoccupied were they with their misfortune that the idea of calling an ambulance never occurred to them. So it was up to me to take charge of things. I felt nothing but coldness and clarity. I was nineteen and yet I acted as prudently as a fifty-year-old; my mind was quite sober. I stood on the solid ground of truth that had suddenly appeared in our house, and I said to myself: Now you must take the telephone book, you must look up 'accident' or 'hospital', you must pick up the phone, say something about an accident and call an ambulance. It must come at once, she might still be saved. You must finally look after your sister – now you can do that for the first time.

Of course the whole thing had to be hushed up. When the ambulance rang at the door and the men with the red cross and the long fabric stretcher came clattering up the stairs, my mother hurried into the street where people had gathered around the vehicle with the red cross.

Emergency vehicles very rarely came to Eichkamp. You could be certain that something extraordinary was going on. Once, in 1929, on Lärchenweg, I would have been nine or ten at the time, an elderly spinster had poisoned herself. It must have been gas, because the firemen climbed up the outside walls with a fearsome selection of ladders, clambered about awkwardly on the roof and got inside through some skylight or other. I didn't understand the circumstances, because nothing was visible from outside, everything looked as it always did. My mother had been afraid of gas ever since, and it was then that the routine with the square spanner had begun. Once a couple had killed themselves with sleeping tablets; that was in 1934. They were thought to have been Jews, and terrible things like that did seem to happen to Jews. Once a maid from Kiefernweg had strangled her illegitimate child with a towel. The news ran through our little estate in a flash like an Athenian message of terror, and irrefutably confirmed for us the complete depravity of the lower orders. It was then that my mother dismissed our maid, because she saw her as a danger to us children. She always said: They're all the same, one rabble very much like another. They are all marked by God.

Yes – and now it was our turn. Now the ambulance was parked outside our house at number 35 Im Eichkamp. It was spring 1938, everything was still intact and looked kind and inviting, the walls of the house were covered with Virginia creeper, and pansies were already coming up in the front garden, and while the men upstairs moved my whimpering sister, my mother downstairs was explaining to the people in the street that it was something to do with her appendix, that her daughter had a case of acute and serious appendicitis.

That made sense, and then she ran upstairs and for the first time she carefully wiped the blood from her daughter's face, because of course even the people of Eichkamp knew that appendicitis didn't usually lead to bleeding from the mouth.

Then the ambulance drove away. No one was allowed to go with her. The orderlies had immediately grasped the situation, they might even have sensed that something forbidden was going on, everything must be left as it was, they also had to inform the police. Our green pinewood front door slammed shut, the new security lock snapped into place, and I was suddenly sitting with my parents as if in a mousetrap. Eichkamp imprisonment: now it was obvious. An air of crime, an air of grandeur and destiny had settled upon us all. We sat helplessly in our big club chairs and for the first time we sensed the breath of the big world passing through our cramped rooms. Life was incredible – who would ever have thought it? Now school and the Hitler Youth, and Tacitus' writings about the Teutons, were no longer worth heeding; not the Ministry, Reich Minister Rust* and the many fine laws and decrees of the *völkisch* state, not the art about which my mother was so enthusiastic, Schubert's *Winterreise* and Wagner's *Wesendonck Lieder* – death had suddenly intervened, and we could not cope with its immensity.

We sat there as if time had suddenly stopped. That morning we were like bad amateur actors performing a swiftly improvised *Electra* and *Antigone* in a Berlin back room. Tragedy had moved into our house, and of course we were not a match for the script. My acting was particularly bad. I should have been moved and unhappy. That was what the part called for. She was my sister. But all I felt was a malevolent feeling of triumph: Now there you have it. It's come out now. This is what life is like, just like this.

*

Ursula was delivered to the Westend Hospital. She lived on, in a tough and stubborn way, for another twenty-one days, as she approached the death that she herself had summoned. Death rose slowly upwards from her abdomen, it began between her genitals and her intestines and crept slowly up from there. It was a case of violent poisoning, the doctors explained to us.

Sublimate is highly concentrated mercury, and if a person ingests large quantities of it they are introducing the poison into their stomach and from there into their intestines. There it stays and begins to break down the organism. Sublimate is a universal decomposer, a universal crusher; it turns our flesh to mush and dissolves the organs very slowly into a bloody sludge. Then it rises through the body, and when it reaches the kidneys, the kidneys are dissolved, and then they are unable to filter out urine. The urine remains in the body and builds up, and when the urine reaches the heart, the heart stops and it's over. That is called uraemia, and it usually happens very quickly, but in Ursula's case it took a long time. She took three weeks, and those three weeks allowed us very slowly to grasp the disaster, to come to terms with the calamity. Death requires style, style wanted to form – who could ever understand death without style?

The shadow of criminality had quickly faded from our house. My father had telephoned the police from the Ministry, the Westend Hospital had telephoned my father, and then the police had telephoned the Westend Hospital again. The matter was now running along official tracks which quickly and completely exonerated us. Admittedly the rumour of appendicitis did not survive for long in Eichkamp. Some things had seeped through. Certain admissions had to be made, initially vague and ambiguous; an arrangement had to be reached. My mother now spoke often of the blow that fate had dealt us, and when one day she suddenly admitted over lunch: 'The poor child, our Ursel, how she must have suffered!' she was on the right path.

Life slowly re-established itself in our house. Everyday life wanted to reclaim its rights. I went to school again, prepared myself for the Abitur, wrote a long essay about Hans Grimm and the 'völkische Lebensraum',* my father travelled again to the Ministry of Culture at 8.23 and brought home lots of files about art, and my mother now cooked with greater care and produced tastier meals than ever before. And in the afternoon we went in turn to the Westend Hospital and visited our dying child: only twenty-one years old. It was a moving expansion of our Lebensraum. Never had we left Eichkamp so frequently. There was something missing at home, that was certain, but on the other hand we now had a bright and high-ceilinged room in Charlottenburg that clearly bore the thrill of another world. We took the suburban train, but those train journeys were more like quiet pilgrimages to Lourdes or Konnersreuth. My mother now spoke often of Therese, and I never knew if she meant the one from Avila, the one from Lisieux or the one from Konnersreuth.* The mystery of the blood preoccupied us, the mystery of suffering cried out for resolution, and the books of Chaplain Fahsel were now joined by accounts of the Konnersreuth case. In that instance they had learned how easily suffering in girls can involve blood. It was a *mysterium*, as I was often told. The word was new to me. I looked it up in the dictionary and saw that the matter was, quite surprisingly, taking a religious turn.

Ursula's sick room was, in fact, little suited to spiritual transfiguration. It was in the women's section, ward B, fifth floor, room 23. Everything in the Westend Hospital had the whiff of doctors; at reception you had to awkwardly identify yourself, you had to stick meticulously to the visiting hours and do battle with cantankerous nurses, and the floor upstairs was polished until it was so bright and shiny that you had to take great care as you walked along it. Ursula was in a high white enamel bed, strangely packed and wrapped up. Lots of devices stood around her bed, lots of jars on these devices were connected to her bed by brown tubes. Clearly she was being artificially fed, and had to be artificially emptied as well. The whole hidden sphere of the abdomen, which in our house had always been considered as low and dirty, had now become art, the pure art of the doctors, and beneath this artifice her face blossomed with charm and beauty. She lay there as if in ecstasy; now she was able to speak a little again. Words issued quietly and intermittently from her scabbed mouth, and like all suicides who return to life she now regretted what she had done. She showed a mute determination to reverse the whole process and the doctors confirmed that hope for her: Definitely, quite certainly, in three or four weeks she would be back home, perhaps in a wheelchair; that possibility could not be discounted for the time being.

So Ursula went through a distinct phase of regeneration, and that period of vital recovery gave my mother a bright idea. She had decided that Ursula must convert. That Monday, she said one day over dinner, had been a clear hint from heaven. Many things had been ignored in our family, many things criminally neglected ever since her marriage. She had married as a Catholic without the blessing of her Church, and the room in which Ursula was dying in Charlottenburg was now giving her the powerful piece of moral superiority that was so urgently required for the correction of such early and grievous errors.

My father was essentially indifferent to such things. He had no interest in religion in this respect or any other. It was probably his mother who had, in the manner of stubborn old Protestants, demanded that spiritual humiliation of her Catholic daughter-in-law. That was a long time ago, the day war broke out in 1914. His Protestant mother was dead now, her remains had lain in Buckow in the Märkische Schweiz since 1931, and Catholicism, long suppressed, was now suddenly dominant in response to our disaster. There was much revising to be done.

So on the afternoons when she wasn't visiting, my mother went in search of spiritual support. This proved to be an extremely delicate matter. On the one hand, my mother insisted that they had to be gentlemen of the better kind, high-ranking dignitaries and if possible members of priestly orders, not profane secular priests who led an ordinary and dubious worldly life with their housekeepers and members of their Berlin congregations; on the other hand, those gentlemen with theological pedigree were the very ones who proved most intransigent. The cathedral prelates and monsignors to whom my mother effortlessly gained access, the heads of spiritual orders and padres always twitched a little when, after some well-spoken words, they heard the term 'suicide'. That was a difficult matter, she was informed. The Church, the Holy Mother, required of their children full spiritual clarity for such a grave step and sound health was also required. There was talk of a complete conversion, of complete penance and mercy. It was clear that the senior-ranking gentlemen had no intention of presenting themselves as a pious firm of undertakers. Even Thomas Aquinas had …

But meanwhile my mother had been busy too. In the evening hours, when she had previously opened the local newspaper, she thumbed pious books and happened upon a quotation that she now used to back up her position. She had bought Saint Augustine's *Confessions* in a pocket edition

– at a cost of two marks eighty – and she read it attentively in the evening. There she had happened upon a quotation that seemed apt, like a key to the heart of the Church and her daughter. The phrase was 'Restless is our heart until it comes to rest in Thee, O Lord!' That poor child, our Ursel, she now liked to say. Her restless heart. She was fundamentally in search of God.

It really was apt. I don't know how many churches and chapels, monastic houses and church offices between Friedrichstrasse and Grunewald my mother hurried to in those days. She proved extraordinarily active and proficient in matters pertaining to the Church. One evening she came home at around six o'clock with an air of quiet triumph, contentedly put her black handbag inside our baroque cabinet, turned the heavy key twice, pulled it out and locked it in the drawer of my father's desk, pulled that key out as well, put it in our sideboard and, as she locked the sideboard too, declared that it had all been sorted out. Father Ambrosius of the Salesians would be looking in at the hospital the next day.

Father Ambrosius was a kindly, bald man with a slight but barely noticeable outward squint. He wore a black habit, and a small cap on the top of his head, kept his eyes lowered and came from somewhere near Zehlendorf – his order's Mother House was in Freilassing near Salzburg. He was not really distinguished enough for our case, and he also seemed to lack a sense of spiritual vocation. He showed a curious kind of theological stubbornness and wanted to start out with a clumsy conversion class; he brought his catechism and instructed the dying child from Eichkamp about the whence and whither and what-for and why of the world in general, about the intentions of the Creator, which were essentially good and pure, and how differently things had turned out because of Eve.

My mother was irritated by this. No fuss, she sometimes said crossly, just get on with it – the spirit is all that matters. She was probably on the left wing of the Church, and even then rebelled against the cool rationalism of the Thomist healing apparatus. 'Mercy,' she said, 'all that matters is mercy!' In fact there was no time to lose. Her daughter was still blooming a little from the artificial feeding and evacuation, but the redness and beauty of her face were already shadowed by the dark grace of death. And just as a spiritual man was beginning to take charge of her regime the doctors slowly withdrew their assistance and said sadly that things could be over any day now. They had done everything they could. Then another doctor must come, my mother exclaimed, meaning not Father Ambrosius but Jesus himself. We were swimming in a sea of religiosity.

On 11 April – it was a Tuesday, ten o'clock in the morning – the other doctor did come. Room 23 had been transformed into a little blossoming chapel. It no longer smelled of doctors, it smelled entirely of Catholicism. A lot of flowers in the room, pictures of saints on the wall, a little holy water stoup beside the door. In the corner an actual altar had been set up with candles and a crucifix, and Father Ambrosius brought the little bit of altar stone, the martyr's bone required by Roman custom, in a black leather bag which, like an overnight bag, was filled very practically with all kinds of religious utensils for every eventuality. From this case he took the sacred implements required for the administration of baptism, followed by confession, followed by a mass with holy communion followed by extreme unction. I was surprised and startled by so many rituals from Zehlendorf. Four sacraments were being administered at once, and if my mother had been elevated to the rank of bishop and allowed to choose, there might also have been a confirmation. The mercy was boundless; it broke like a torrent over the sinner from Eichkamp and washed her miraculously clean. As it did so Father Ambrosius sang, exchanged words with an altar boy, donned new garments, trickled water over Ursel's brow, placed a stole and books at the ready, prayed for a long time and later mixed an oil, and in between there was a lot of incense and bell-ringing and candlelight. Tears were also appropriate now. Tears of grief and beatitude.

We all had to go outside for a while. Confession was probably being heard, and I tried to imagine what she would be saying right now. How often she had stolen and secretly snacked, how often she had been badly behaved and had immodest thoughts. It was unimaginable. I stood by the corridor window and stared rigidly at the traffic in the street. The people down there were walking as if nothing had happened: housewives and Brownshirts, lots of young Luftwaffe soldiers and elderly men, some with dogs. Charlottenburg went on living. Now my mother was holding a rosary and sobbing occasionally. We didn't know if we were at a wedding or a funeral, but strictly speaking it was a baptism, the celebration of a second birth, though in our particular case a celebration of blissful grief. Even Father Ambrosius had spoken of *felix culpa*. So everything turned out well in the end, and he had quoted a poet unfamiliar to us: Every torment leaves us richer, praise be to sacred hardship!

She is dead, she is dead, she fell blissfully asleep yesterday. She could not fight against the evil poison, she could not struggle against pious transfiguration. Now she lies there: rigid, stiff and white, and an odour of sanctity emanates from her. She went ahead of all of us, and now she will rise to heaven. Her eyes are piously closed, her mouth is closed, a rosary has been wrapped around her clasped hands like a tender manacle – a manacle of love, no one will free her of it. She has been transformed by the balm of faith into a Bride of Christ, and yet there she lies like a heavy parcel of silence, wrapped and sealed and tenderly tied. That is how the daughters of Egyptian kings lie on their biers, turned into masks of eternity with wood and paint, with wax and bandages. They have wrapped and sealed you, they have embellished you with the bandages of faith. They have transfigured you and now they will jerkily haul you up on to the gallows of faith like Saint Joan of the Stockyards for her final triumph.* A Deutsche Oper performance in Charlottenburg – on the left the Church and on the right the bourgeoisie, and both will now join in with the celebration in stirring choruses: death and transfiguration, the haloing and canonisation of the little saint from Eichkamp.

Just cling on tightly to these straps, otherwise everything will fall apart. Everything within you is broken, your body has dissolved, your kidneys are pulp and have flooded your heart with urine, it began between your intestines and your genitals. Why don't you say it? Say it: It was never true, it was all terrible, it was terrifying, and life with you a constant torture. Why don't you say it: This soil was bad, it was exhausted, it was rotten and mouldy; only these poisonous mushrooms of death can grow from Eichkamp's houses now. There was so much fear in you, and you were always alone. Everything was so cramped, so rigid, as if strapped firmly in place. And later, when you grew older, you felt something like love within you and didn't know what to do with it. Repugnant experience at seventeen: not knowing what to do with it. You were walled in, incarcerated in the prison of your body, you felt love and didn't know where to take it. There was no pole that attracted it, no direction that it wanted to go in, no window through which one could look out and see it. There was no door in Eichkamp that could be pushed open. Everything within you was closed. You drowned in that youth of yours, you suffocated, your strength used up. Perhaps you needed a husband and lots of children, that might have been a way out, but you could no longer escape yourself – that world outside, that father, that mother, they weren't what you wanted. I understand that. It must be a release to die if it means escaping such prisons. It must have been a hope, the first time you saw that tube with the death's head. I can imagine it: a monstrous hope that something would happen now. So nothingness rises from the depths, it battles its way like damp through the walls of the generations, it eats its way into the flesh of the children and suddenly it breaks out; it is called a tragedy, but for us it became more of a family celebration, a mediocre comedy of kinship.

The day after my sister's death my mother sat down at our little black-painted desk and informed the public of what had happened to us. She telephoned newspapers and print-shops, she posted off precise announcements, she had lots of black-rimmed missives printed to bear our misfortune swiftly into the world. She had ordered three requiems and invited our relatives to the funeral. In spite of everything it was to be a feast of mercy.

Together with Father Ambrosius my parents had reached the verdict that Ursula had gone to eternity in the honourable state of virginity. Even in those days people were complaining that this was becoming increasingly rare. So she belonged with the innocent children. She was a *virgo intacta*, as my mother was able to establish with clerical assistance, and for a long time I didn't understand why she was now

using that strange phrase all the time. She told the neighbours and the doctors, she spread it about at the florist's and
informed the stonemasons that this was a special case of
an *intacta*. Obviously she had never been sullied. The word
sounded strange to my ears. I knew extractors and reactors. I
heard all the hard A's in these words as sharp hammer-blows,
and had to look through the dictionary for a long time
before I worked out that this was not something to do with
technology.

In fact, the advantages were impressive. Father Ambrosius
had referred us to the honourable custom of the Church that
virgines intactae were seen as innocent children before the
Lord, and therefore, like real children, could lay claim to
a white burial. Here only joy and heavenly jubilation were
appropriate, and the fact of the white coffin and the virgin's
wreath with its silver decoration on it moved us deeply and
made us reflective. Now it had been proven how rewarding it
was not to sleep with men. Ursula would sleep her way into
eternity blissful and white, almost like a nun. And again the
poet's word was quoted: Praise be to sacred hardship!

A few days later all the people that we had invited turned
up. They came from Grünberg and Neuzelle, from Glogau
and Glatz and, along with black-draped hats and fat suitcases, they brought with them a lot of Silesian sympathy.
Uncle Hans and Aunt Anna from Neuzelle brought to Berlin
a smell of cinnamon and conviviality from their grocer's
shop on Adolf Hitler Strasse. From Grünberg came Uncle
Osswald, known as Sour Ossi, because the sour Grünberg
wine to which he was secretly addicted had given him the
careworn yet cheery face of a bachelor. The more elegant
Flickschuhs from Frankfurt an der Oder came, who lived
in a permanent feud with their parish priest and engaged
in a significant correspondence about it with the relevant

ordinariate. And Hermann the schoolteacher came with his wife Gertrude from Glatz; they had ten children at home. And they were all Catholic, they seemed warm and plump, they set their suitcases down imperiously in our narrow corridor, looked at the walls searching for holy water stoups, which we didn't have, and urgently demanded to see the one who had prematurely passed away.

Then the Protestants came from the North. Aunt Alma came from Stettin, a thin and elderly former postal employee who spoke the Saxon dialect and who had wisely taken early retirement from her job as a telephone operator in her mid-thirties. Since then she had lived on an incredibly tiny pension, alone with her cat, had turned the miserliness of an old maid into a high art, adding to it the pride of having been one of the first female civil servants in Germany, and was constantly telling us that our lives were far too wasteful. At that time she was collecting tin foil and used paper for the Wehrmacht; without thrift, she said, no state could flourish. Then Uncle Hans and Aunt Eva came from Hamburg-Eidelstedt: Herr and Frau Corvette Captain, who still bore the aura of their tropical adventures – they had yellow, leathery skin and looked very tough and sharp, and demonstrated a streak of Hanseatic hard-headedness. All day they chain-smoked nervously, and spread an alien, spicy smell of worldliness around our poky rooms. They didn't look for holy water stoups, they demanded whisky. Aunt Alma found it all very wasteful.

And both family lines, wrapped in their black Sunday best, eyed each other suspiciously; hitherto they had only heard of one another and were, so to speak, lying in wait to see which would be the first to offer their weak spot to the other. In spite of the larger numbers, the Catholics were noticeably inferior. There was something slovenly and rascally about them. They probably had too much heart and too little in their heads, and the Protestants, who were the other way around, made them feel this with little mocking turns of phrase. But Uncle Hans from Neuzelle and Uncle Hans from Hamburg also shared a common bond. They were both Party members, for one thing, one out of loyalty, the other out of conviction. For the funeral they wore their Party badges proudly on the right lapels of their coats, lest anyone in the big city think they were just anybody. It seemed to me during those days that the swastika worn by Uncle Hans the Catholic looked much friendlier and more trustworthy. With Uncle Hans the Protestant, it was a different symbol. On him it looked cold and strange and Northern. He had spent the Weimar Republic in Java, and was now once again an officer in a U-boat school.

And now they all populated our little house, which was suddenly full of life and bustle. They demanded bed sheets, blankets and chamber pots, they wanted to read newspapers and listen to the radio, they spoke occasionally of the return of Austria to the Reich, and how the Führer's youthful dream had been finally fulfilled in Vienna. In the meantime wreaths were brought and garlands with big ribbons delivered to the house. So much pine-tree foliage made everything smell Christmassy, and in the meantime my mother accepted visits of condolence in the study. Aunt Alma slept in Ursula's bed, and I had to move into the kitchen because the elegant Flickschuhs, the ones who corresponded with the ordinariate, wanted to sleep in my room.

It turned into a long and unforgettable family celebration, whose climax as so often in such cases did not come until after the funeral. People usually go somewhere for a funeral feast, but my mother, along with a maid and Aunt Alma, had set everything up at home. It was part of the spirit of the family not to engage purely commercially with strangers outside. We had always lived quietly and alone in Eichkamp. My mother had previously responded to every announcement of a visit from a relative with a hasty dispatch informing them – unfortunately – that she was currently unwell. So over many years no one had made it as far as our house. We had lived as if in a besieged city, a closed society, and kept only our own company. That was over now. The fortress had been taken, the gate was open, and family flowed in over Ursula's deathbed from everywhere, thronging down all the corridors, occupying all the rooms, lingering in the kitchen, climbing the stairs, going out into the garden, standing outside the front door. Family spilled from every nook and cranny and created a very confined space. It was now that I learned the joy of brotherly love, the consoling power of the wider family, from which we are sadly moving ever further away.

At about five in the afternoon the feast reached its peak. Our dining table had been pulled out to accommodate a small banquet, which by now threatened to head for a wild and enjoyable dénouement. Wine glasses and coffee cups stood around at random. Never had our dining room been so glittering, so festive and extravagant. The fine crystal glasses and the Meissen porcelain, the asparagus plates and silver plates which had for decades stiffly adorned our sideboard as an artful display, and which had been dusted countless times, were now put to reckless use. Ursula's death gave them life. The black-leather-covered canteens of cutlery, from whose red cushions the silver knives and forks had been awakened from decades of sleep, were now open in the kitchen. It became apparent that we were considerably affluent. My parents' wedding presents were put to use for the first time in twenty-four years: heavy silver napkin rings with the date 1914 engraved in old-fashioned swirls. There were ladles gilded on the inside with monograms that I had never seen before, and lots of heavy crystal pudding bowls that my mother now released from long-locked cupboards.

Uncle Hans, the Catholic, was in a melancholy red-wine mood. His pain was muted, his grief transfigured; as always after a good dinner, there was a mood of quiet reflection. There was also the fact that he was sitting directly opposite Father Ambrosius, who had been unable to resist my mother's pleas, and had come to us briefly at least. And now the pious Salesian sat within our walls like a little clerical show-piece, he sat humbly by my mother's side, as she had always dreamed he might. They sat there harmoniously, as Francis and Clare once sat in Assisi, and everything would probably have been fine, had not Uncle Hans suddenly risen to his feet. He stood up with a clumsy and spluttering gesture, revealing a heavy gold chain across his belly, with three brownish stags' teeth dangling from it. His face was red and glistening with festive perspiration. He wiped his face with his crumpled napkin, tapped his glass, set down his cigar and then raised his glass with his right hand. 'Father,' I heard him saying in a deep and gurgling voice, 'let us remember our dear beloved, who is now in heaven – by your help.' Then he set his glass down, rummaged in his trouser pocket, took out a shiny brown wallet, flicked through it and took out a bank-note: fifty marks, which he displayed to the gathering for a moment, with a combination of confidentiality and triumph. Then he set the note down humbly on Father Ambrosius's cake plate, laid a cake fork on top of it and said: 'Father: a requiem for Ursula.'

Father Ambrosius was no doubt about to turn this gift modestly down, but he didn't get a chance, because suddenly something happened to me. I must have silently collapsed, and crashed my head against a little crystal plate that jumped sideways with a clatter and danced merrily for a while on our wooden floor. I had a raging cramp inside me, my whole stomach was constricted, retching and lurching upwards. My torso bent forward, and I must have lost consciousness for a second, because when I came to I saw that I had vomited across the table. There was a damp brown substance on the white linen, and it immediately reminded me of the blood on my sister's pillow. The brown colour seeped slowly in, forming concentric circles, and when I noticed the sour taste in my mouth I was startled: blood, I thought, only blood can taste like this. I pulled myself up, knocked my chair over and ran blindly out – out of the dining room, out of the kitchen, I ran into the garden and stopped somewhere near a wooden bench.

The silence of a spring evening lay over the gardens. There was a smell of fresh grass, and there were blue pansies in full bloom. In our neighbour's garden someone was watering beds with young lettuce, flocks of sparrows were already drifting across the broad blue sky, and somewhere a bright and joyful 'ding' rang out from a cyclist's bell. A peaceful Eichkamp evening. Then I see the kitchen door opening and my mother coming out, followed by Uncle Hans the Catholic, her brother. She is leaning on his arm. They are both draped in black and getting closer and closer to me. I can't avoid them, I can't get away, I can't undo things. I taste blood in my mouth. Here comes the family, your family. They will kill you. They have seen me, they're getting ever closer. And I hear my mother saying to her brother: 'But Hans, she was his sister after all.' And I think: Yes, that's right, of course, she was your sister.

And at that thought I feel suddenly something within me shattering, breaking, collapsing: my pride, my arrogance and my coldness. For the first time in three weeks that evil, terrible rigidity leaves me. For the first time I feel pain, real, simple pain. Everything suddenly begins to slip and slide. I feel dizzy. There's an abyss before me. I fall and fall, deeper and deeper, I fall down the shafts of the past – soon I'm going to hit the bottom. I'm a child again, I want to weep like a child, cry like a child, be sad like a child, I want to be like all the other children too.

MY FRIEND WANJA

Prague, they say, is a beautiful city. Is Prague a beautiful city? They say it is. They say: even today Prague is a beautiful city, particularly now, particularly now again when so many things are starting to change. Golden, eternal Prague, baroque and Catholic, monumental and charming, the city on the Vltava, the crown of art: go to Prague – it's still a magical city. The word 'magical' should have aroused my suspicions.

Do you know Prague? I felt about Prague as I always do about cities that you end up visiting after hearing about them for years: at first there's only disappointment. You arrive in the afternoon, and it's always a Sunday afternoon, and on Sunday afternoons all the cities in the world are hell for strangers. You can't get in anywhere, it's usually raining, and everything is decaying solemnly away, because it's Sunday after all. Of course you arrived with certain expectations: golden Prague, baroque and Catholic and still magical. On this occasion I got everything wrong. You walk through the streets, which are empty and drenched with rain. You go to Wenceslas Square and you keep looking out for the fortress, the castle and St Vitus' Cathedral, and you cross lots of wet bridges over the Vltava, with saints and angels on either side, as marmoreally cold as in a thousand churches.

Prague has lots of palaces and noblemen's houses, that's probably true, but on this occasion it left me cold; back then everything conspired against me, the windows were closed, the gates held their interiors firmly locked to me. The city was very empty and terribly drained of work, life and trade; it looked as beautiful and boring as a front room: a room for visitors with lace tablecloths and lots of knick-knacks. That was my Prague: a feeling of walls, of stone and curved emptiness, a flavour of pointlessness and disappointment. It was quite a mad, sick feeling.

Do you recognise that distinctive and devious temptation to crank up that state of disappointment in a nauseating way? Of course you have long been trapped within your own depths. The path outside is closed. Of course you always have a few addresses in your pocket, two or three telephone numbers; people like us never travel without them. Now you should make that call. You don't do it. You're so in love with that feeling of disappointment, savouring that feeling. There is a malicious hope in you that you can turn your disappointment into a major event: pack your bags the next morning and go home. I've been there, but you'll never know. I've been there, but I couldn't get in, because in fact I wasn't really there. I just walked along the streets and squares, over the bridges and up and down the steps of Prague and then I left again. I was afraid, afraid of starting, afraid of calling, afraid of saying: Here I am, I'm here. I couldn't cope with Prague that time. I was deeply immersed in my fear and loneliness. I came from the West and brought with me a sense of decay and a refined way of life.

For such cases there is only one solution in the whole world: Roma Termini, Gare du Nord, Waterloo station. All the railway stations in the world are crammed full of expectation, disappointment and ruined happiness. You can draw

on that. Among brightly coloured kiosks and dusty track clo-
sures life goes on; you can pick it up again and then find your
way back. At railway stations there are train tracks, timeta-
bles and fixed tariffs; dependable things that you can cling on
to. And more importantly there are all the other people who
also went to the station because they had the same experience. Every station concourse is a collection of people who
have somehow got lost or been thrown off the train, a meet-
ing-place of the lonely and the mad. You can smell the expectation and the hope, because all lonely people run around
like animals, and sniff at each other like animals, and pretend
that something exists outside that is in fact going on inside:
the state of being lost. It has quite a repellent odour.

My place of refuge at that time was a newspaper kiosk. They
have far fewer papers in Prague than they do in Germany, so
a newspaper kiosk looks distinctly more pallid and plain: the
front pages of the papers are free of seductive sin, the thrill
of depravity. Still, they do have newspapers, and I bought
myself one because I said to myself: You might be able to
make a phone call later. I bought myself *Neues Deutschland*.*
It's not a paper that sets my pulse racing particularly. It's just
too official and stiff and reminds me too much of *l'Osserva-
tore Romano* or the Limburg *Bonifatiusboten*: it's all so stiff,
it speaks down to the reader. But if you're in Prague and you
don't understand the language of the city, and it's Sunday
afternoon and it's drizzling away, and you feel utterly pointless, you can pick up something like that and say to yourself:
Still, other people have to read this every day. It can't hurt.

No, I'm not going to tell you how I finally did manage to
force my way into the city, to conquer it and find it as beautiful as all the guidebooks say it is. I just want to say that on
that horribly misfired Sunday evening I was already in bed
at half past nine, and that's when it happened. That's when it

happened. Hotel beds under socialism aren't bad. Of course everything's a bit old-fashioned and heavy. But doesn't that give you a sense of security? It's like visiting your aristocratic grandmother in the country: everything is very proper and tastefully bourgeois; they still have decent linen hand towels, none of that new German junk, all those pull-out beds and plastic showers that you get in Düsseldorf or Frankfurt, where we catch our neuroses.

I had lit myself a cigar and slugged down the remains of a Western whisky from a thin hip flask. I was a journalist from the West who had come to socialist Prague in April 1963, with his eccentricities, his arrogance, his cigars and hip flasks and his middle-aged neuroses, in the hope of finding everything good and progressive. What's wrong with that?

Even then *Neues Deutschland* was reporting on the dazzling successes of socialism in the Middle East, particularly in Egypt, where the Americans had been getting up to one of their indescribably stupid interventions again. That too had infuriated *Neues Deutschland*, and now they were writing about it on the front page under a big banner headline. And I read the first line, which said: 'As our Middle East correspondent Lothar Killmer reports from Cairo …'

News pages all over the world start with such banal introductory phrases. Agency reports, correspondent reports: dpa and Reuter's and UPI and TASS – you just skim those passages, and so you should, and I did too for a few seconds, but not more. The name struck me. Names sometimes have an indescribable penetrating power. Scientists call it 'threshold excitation' or indeed the 'disintegration effect'. I saw only the name, even though it was not unusual in any way, I read it again and again and suddenly I knew: it was there once, it was there once in your life. Of course – it could be him. So you fall back, you slip down the shafts of time as swiftly as in a lift, down to the bottom, where there's only your childhood: thick and touching and mushy. And suddenly, with an indescribable surge of childish emotion, I realised: of course, that could be Wanja. Now at last you have a trace of him – after twenty years.

Herr Focken was our classics teacher. He was an old-style Prussian man of culture: he was swathed in an aura of humanist helplessness and Protestant inwardness when he entered our classroom with a shamefaced 'Heil Hitler'. He tried to get it out of the way as quickly as possible. He wore ankle gaiters and tight green woodman's suits with high-fitting pockets. That made him look – he was already in his late fifties at the time – both solidly German and ancient: the thinness of his legs and the feebleness of his Protestant torso were made very much apparent in these quaint robes. Herr Focken was our classics teacher; he was the man who taught us all the quaint sayings, the elevated waffle of the cultured German bourgeoisie that we call the imperishable legacy: from Xenophon to Erasmus, from Tacitus to Luther, from the Protestant hymnbook to the Brothers Grimm, he found everything profound and serious and noteworthy, and he persuaded us to feel the same. He also liked to sing; as late as 1936 he opened our Latin class in a high, brave voice: 'Lord, Thy goodness lasts for ever'. He sang in a lonely, confident voice, holding his hands clasped together against his body, firmly and yet with the fingers somewhat splayed. His right eye had a slight light-blue outward squint, so that you never knew quite where he was looking when he sang like that; but his eyes were always directed upwards.

Herr Focken's relationship with the new state was expressed in the single sentence with which whole generations of

Germans had been cheerfully sent to their graves: *Mens sana in corpore sano*. Herr Focken was equally in favour of Plato, Luther and Walter Flex.* He had fought as a volunteer in the First World War, cheerful and God-fearing, as he put it, and strengthened by his brand of German introspection. 'Lads,' he sometimes said, twisting his mouth into a grimace of wild pedagogical determination that made us boys secretly giggle. 'Lads, think of Walter Flex: a healthy mind can only dwell in a healthy body!' We could almost hear all his limbs cracking as he pulled himself resolutely up.

One day Herr Focken did not come alone. How can I ever forget it? It was in Berlin, it was in the autumn of 1936, shortly after the Olympic Games, it was in fifth year at the Grunewald Gymnasium, now called the Walther Rathenau School, because Walther Rathenau was shot just around the corner on the Königsallee – we knew nothing of that at the time.* Herr Focken came with a stack of black exercise books, he came with his hymnbook under his arm and he came with Wanja. Wanja looked like Kaspar Hauser, only slightly smaller.* They were an incredibly comical-looking sight as they suddenly stood in the doorway and tried to say: 'Heil Hitler.' The exercise books slipped out from under Herr Focken's arm; twenty-nine black dictation books clattered to the floor and the new boy pounced on them like a weasel to resolve the situation as quickly as possible. He flapped both arms around in the pile, pushed everything together and dropped everything again, and he did so with a gesture of breathless goodwill that seemed a parody of its own point-lessness: the devil had arrived, the rogue and creator of chaos had come. 'A new boy,' Herr Focken said, stepping elegantly over the black pile with his thin legs and opening his hymn-book. Then he sang with his eyes fixed on the ceiling. Now he was singing for Lothar Killmer as well.

The new boy was short, broad and swarthy; he had a stout, squat body and short, strong limbs. His hair hung tousled over his face and was shaggy at the back of his neck; he had a big liver stain on his throat. He was completely unkempt. He seemed to come from another world. In the context of our grammar school he seemed extremely coarse. In those days most of the students at our school were very elegant and well dressed, upper class, scions of the Prussian bourgeoisie, smooth-mannered, and with an air of shallow gentleman-liness even at the age of sixteen. Sons of manufacturers, of magistrates and officers, who would later, like their fathers, go riding for an hour in the morning or play tennis, and meet for gentlemen's evenings at the Roseneck after work. Grunewald was very elegant at the time: waterfront proper-ties with big parks and old villas around the Hasensprung – Protestant, Prussian, and with something of the Junker about them. It was probably the last moment of that class that would be doomed to destruction on 20 July 1944. They were the 'elite', as we would say, and I did not belong with them. I noticed that very quickly. I belonged with the new boy. I knew that one day I would belong with him. He had been with us for barely three or four weeks, and we had shared a desk for all that time. I had whispered the answers when he was examined about boring old Xenophon, when the new boy passed me a note, on which was written: 'My name is Wanja, don't tell anybody.' It was then that I realised that he would be the friend of my youth.

Do we know what friendship really is? What is it? Something comes together, things unite, things outwardly separated are inwardly bound. We always seek in the other our own possibility, the one that we do not live ourselves. Wanja was my other possibility, which I would never have had the strength to live. He was opposed to order in a way that was unthinkable at the time. I only found this out slowly, and it attracted me. He was completely different to everyone else, and had more or less all the shortcomings that one could have in Berlin-Grunewald under Adolf Hitler: he came from a proletarian background, he was half-Jewish and half-Russian, and his mother, as the von Kleists and von Mansteins giggled secretly at breaktime, was a worker, a Fräulein, a worker Fräulein from Halensee. For a while the rumour circulated that he was the illegitimate offspring of the Soviet Commissar for Foreign Affairs, Litvinov. This rumour was fanciful. We never resolved it either way. He refused to tell me anything about his father. Wanja's father was his Achilles heel. I would only realise that much later.

Wanja was the outsider incarnate. He didn't fit in anywhere, and yet from that destiny he had created a wonderful position of independence. He was completely free, and took a grim pleasure in the joys of freedom. He enjoyed being alive, he enjoyed existing, he enjoyed making what he wanted of the world. He was healthy, strong and magnificently simple – any doubts or questions he solved with a grin, just as he might have pulled a face. He loved life, he went swimming, rowing and boxing. Even at the age of seventeen he had a girlfriend whom he slept with at weekends. On Monday mornings we met at Halensee station at half-past seven. Then he would arrive, always a little late, always tired and somewhat dishevelled, and tell me, as we set off together for school, about the various joys of early married life; what he liked in women and what he didn't. There was a certain connoisseurship in all of this, and then, when we were already on the school steps, he moved on to the subject of Trotsky and reported on a secret conspiracy between Trotsky and Hitler. It was all far removed from my life. I walked beside him in silence, listened to his dark sounds and was afraid of Latin class and afraid of Greek – we were eighteen at the time.

Wanja became, for me, an adventure in which I was deeply involved. He had so much life that I couldn't reach. He was simply there, completely there. He would not be deterred by anything from finding life beautiful. He was actually ugly, but the strength that he brought to it only made him all the more masculine. He wasn't intelligent, and even by then his education was patchy, but he knew what mattered at any given moment, and in delicate situations he would ask our teachers, whom he despised, surprising and reckless counter-questions that threw them into confusion. 'All well and good, you're very clever,' he sometimes said to me, 'but you lack the best thing.' 'The best thing,' I asked, 'what is that?' 'Desire,' he said, and I said, 'Desire for what?' 'For madness,' he said. 'For madness?' 'Yes,' he said, 'you need a bit of it, you need a bit of crazy desire to be here.'

Of course I became devoted to him. I fell under his thrall slowly and inescapably – only at eighteen can you fall so helplessly under someone's thrall. Later you don't give yourself up so completely. When I went to visit him I gave myself up. It was always a journey into another world; I could only look on with astonishment.

Wanja lived behind Halensee station on Westfälische Strasse in a dark and shabby house to the rear of a tenement block. I had never been to such streets before. Everything smelled of poverty and old age. Heavy, creaking doors, worn steps, a smell of coal in the house; you had to climb four storeys and you found yourself standing in front of a blind, old-fashioned glass door that had lots of visiting cards fastened to it with pins. An elderly man grumpily opened the door and eyed me suspiciously. In the corridor, frayed carpets hung over the doors to the rooms. There were musical instruments and tobacco-pipes on the dirty walls. A smell from the kitchen, a woman's voice sang, and then Wanja stepped out from behind one of those frayed carpets. He was in a bizarre disguise. He wore a red Russian smock with a daring neckerchief, and short green trousers, his sockless feet were in felt slippers and he said, 'Come on, come in here,' said it in an inviting yet strange voice, as if he hadn't been sharing a desk with me that very morning. Here he was someone else, he was strange and mysterious, and he led me into a realm that I didn't know, which enticed and frightened me. He was completely different here. It was like an opium den for the poor. Nothing but bare floorboards, chests, frayed fabrics, cushions, scraps of carpet and lots of well-thumbed books on the floor. There was no table, no chair; everything was just spread out on the floor. A world to squat, lie and sleep in. Something bedlike was set up below the window: a mattress with a lot of pillows and untidy blankets lay on the bare floor. A samovar bubbled in the corner.

Wanja's world was a quirky mixture of Russian anarchism and the old Berlin proletariat. In the midst of Hitler's rule he still lived here, with his mother, in the wild, romantic-prole-tarian style of the 1920s. His room was a stage of private social revolution. I had never believed that such a thing existed in Germany. I would never have considered it possible that something like this could be so near Eichkamp. In our house everything was upright and respectable, bright and elevated and repellently mediocre. Everything was rigid and stiff and empty, one house very much like another, a dry bureaucracy of existence. Here at Wanja's there was wildness, there was chaos, an abyss of mysteries and incomprehensible things – and in those days I couldn't help falling for that abyss.

I visited Wanja more and more often. I did it secretly and with a bad conscience, and more and more I fell under his spell, I fell into the enchanted realm of that reckless misery that promised so much unexplored richness of life. Wanja made tea and lectured me about the culture of tea. He took out an old and ragged paperback and started reading out loud: Okakura Kakuzo – the book of tea. And later he took one of the musical instruments down from the wall in the corridor. It was a balalaika, he explained to me; I had never heard the word. And then he started singing songs that I hadn't heard either and whose lyrics I didn't understand, because they were Russian folk songs. They were dark and melancholy, they were wild and sometimes they had a delicacy that he didn't quite catch. Now Wanja was a long way away from me, he was a horse-rider, a Cossack, a prince, a farmer's son, singing of a foreign homeland, he was a poet singing of far-off revolutions, of civil wars, of flight and hunger and love. It was a strange and alien world. He plucked the strings and quietly translated the occasional line: 'If you, Parasha, will love me, I will feel like a general, yes, like a general.' And a little later he laughed and pushed everything roughly aside, and lit himself a papirosa. The way he bent the little cardboard tube beforehand with his short, plump fingers demonstrated his complete superiority. In his poverty here he was a king.

Of course my parents viewed this friendship with mounting unease. They didn't like seeing their son, who might one day be a cleric or at least an official in the Prussian state, falling in with such undesirables. Wanja was bad company. They found him strange and weird. By now we are nineteen, and about to sit the Abitur. He has grown a bit taller and broader, he already has the hint of a small, wild moustache around his lips and is still unkempt and furry around the neck. We are in my room, which is bright and pale and colourless. I read to him from Nietzsche and Hölderlin and try, with the helpless gestures of idealism, to make my own extravagant bourgeois world clear to him. I talk to him about Zarathustra and the superman, and that we must all evolve beyond ourselves – towards a distant, final possibility. Rilke comes into it somewhere too.*

Wanja squats on the floor; he doesn't like chairs. He smokes cheap shag from a self-carved pipe and stares straight ahead. He is now wearing a blue Russian smock and coarse brown trousers stuck into a kind of high boot that he has cobbled himself. He only smokes and says nothing and sometimes spits, and in that spitting my hopelessness suddenly becomes obvious. Everything is so pointless and empty. What am I saying? There is impotence in my words. I drop Hyperion and Zarathustra, go to the window and hear Wanja beginning to hum his song. He is humming the song he sang before, deep and melancholy: '… yes, I will feel like a general.' I have a feeling of dark torment, a terrible fury. I look at the streets of Eichkamp: all cul-de-sacs, all errors, all wrong turnings, however much you dress them up with Hölderlin and Nietzsche. Eichkamp's streets all lead nowhere, there is no life here, and I suddenly start hating Wanja. I hate him, he makes me feel so helpless and impotent and he is so superior to me. I run away, I run down the stairs. My mother is standing downstairs by the stove in the kitchen, stirring a Silesian soup, and says: 'Do you really have to bring him here all the time? They say he's half-Jewish. My God, son, you're going to plunge us all into disaster.'

The disaster began beautifully and mysteriously, and in fact it was only Wanja's disaster – it affected me only marginally. We are twenty now. We survived Herr Focken and Walter Flex long ago, and school is over. The life for which we have been preparing for so long and so laboriously is now beginning: we're not studying for school now, but for life. My life was in steep ascent at the time. Like all Germans I had high hopes. I began studying philosophy, I read Kant and Hölderlin and Nietzsche, and in the evening I secretly visited Wanja, whom I hated and whom I loved and from whom I couldn't free myself. We're not studying for school, but for life.

Wanja has changed since our Abitur. He has grown more serious, more reticent. There is an air of caginess in his face and when one evening – it's April 1939 – I ring at his door, I know at once: the time of childhood is over.

His flat is quiet. Candles are burning in his room, and as before everything is hazardously scattered at random on the floor. But there is a woman there, she squats on the mattress in the semi-darkness, and I can only tell that she is there by the cigarette smoke drifting slowly up over the mattress. And Wanja says: 'This is Anni Korn', and he says to her: 'So this is him, Musch, take a look at him!'

And then later there was a long dinner that Anni Korn prepared mysteriously behind those fantastical carpets in the corridor. It was a strange, spicy thing that burned my tongue, couscous or something of the kind with a lot of garlic and pepper, and vodka and papirosa cigarettes, and Anni Korn later read something by Gorky. She is blond and thin, a sharp line runs between her mouth and her nose and she actually looks much older. She could even be thirty. In her presence Wanja is quieter and less sure of himself. She has some kind of power over him that I don't know about. There is a bond between them that I can see but can't understand, a bond of quiet, taciturn familiarity that one can sense in all their movements and which excludes me and simply leaves me out. I feel something like disappointment and jealousy.

In the end, just after midnight, she suddenly puts the book away, fetches a briefcase out from under her pillow, sits cross-legged on the mattress, lights another papirosa, suddenly looks at me piercingly, deeply inhales the cigarette smoke before expelling it sharply through her mouth and then says into the darkness: 'You're going to work with us now, yes? You're one of us?' And I don't understand, I have no idea what she means and what she's doing here, and I look helplessly over at Wanja and hear Wanja saying: 'Of course you're going to work for us now. But please don't ask too many questions.'

So it was that in the spring of 1939 – the protectorate of Bohemia and Moravia had just returned to the Reich – I joined an illegal group working against Hitler in the middle of Germany and in the middle of the Third Reich. I was very surprised. I never looked for this, I never asked them. I was never a hero, I just slipped into it. I hated that state, but it would never have occurred to me that anything could be done about it. What came from above always came from above after all: it was fate, decree or mercy. At any rate, it was part of our destiny, as Herr Focken had told us with regard to the heroes of Greece: O Zeus and Demeter, O Proteus and Glaukos, Moira is in you; all is fate – don't you know that? I would never have thought that one could do anything about Hitler; I would never have believed that he was not a destiny. He was as great as the Greek gods, after all, and more powerful.

But I took the letters that Anni Korn later unpacked from the briefcase. They were carefully sealed and tied, twelve or thirteen letters. The envelopes were bright green, they were firmly sealed and unaddressed. They had small numbers in the place where stamps would usually have been fixed; I later had to erase them. And I took the list that she gave me and over the next few days I delivered the letters according to that list and carefully rubbed out the numbers and saw many strange houses. Berlin is as big and as wide as the world and has as many front doors as the world. You could spend your whole life delivering letters. They had chosen me for some kind of courier service. And later the business with the flyers began, the one that quickly finished us all off. One day we were all arrested.

I didn't see Wanja again until two years later. That was in front of the People's Court in Berlin, at number 3 Bellevuestrasse, where many trials against traitors had been held for many years – ours was on the third floor. We have been at war for a long time. Poland, Holland, Belgium and France have fallen. It is the spring of 1941 and our country is filled with a final wave of victory and enthusiasm. Germany is like an addict who is on the point of collapse, who will soon be a little pile of misery, but for now the needle is back in his vein, and once more he feels the furious rush of power. There have been so many blitz campaigns, orgasms of war; it is as if the German people are high on this happiness, hard as steel and high. They say it's Britain's turn now, and they already have a song for the crossing of the Channel; everyone says it's Britain's turn at last, and no one is thinking about Russia, our ally. The whole of Germany is full of flags, full of heroes and uniforms which, as they say, are suffused with glory. The war is a monstrous victory parade passing across Europe. Germany lies like a war-cloud over the Continent and is now building a new Europe of Teutonic magnificence. Here on Bellevuestrasse there is a war on as well: a war on the home front, a war against traitors, spies and saboteurs. I step into the big courtroom on the third floor of the People's Court, blood-red colours come flying towards me, flags, colours, uniforms. I'm in uniform too, I'm wearing the uniform of a paratrooper; I'm a German corporal who's come from France and who's supposed to be making a witness statement against Wanja. They have ordered me here directly from Caen.

Wanja, how am I ever supposed to forget this moment? Where are you? I can't find you. I see only blood-red flags and a lot of uniforms in the room. At the front, on the wall behind the judge's bench, a massive flag is stretched, perhaps fifteen or twenty metres long. Above it floats a silver imperial eagle, sharp and narrow. Beneath it twelve men sit at a long table, also covered in red cloth, and three of the men are in civilian clothes. The twelve are the judges, I hear, and the three are said to be legal experts; the rest are the People who are to deliver the verdict. On either side of the courtroom broad rows of seats have been set up as in a theatre: Party and Wehrmacht officials sit there, the gentlemen from the internal leadership who have to attend such trials every day to learn the enemy's techniques and tricks in a timely fashion. They are supposed to protect the people against the enemies of the people. They are here to watch a play being performed; it is called 'Wanja and his girlfriend', it is called 'Lothar Killmer and Anni Korn'. A state theatre of power, in which they are all silent and have their heads lowered and stare straight ahead and only one person is shouting. This is what is known here as a hearing.

And then all of a sudden I spot him: he's sitting there small and pale and slumped on a bench to the side, and the woman beside him must be Anni Korn. After two years in prison they are barely recognisable, they have become so small and white and mute. Their heads seem shrunken and from the distance rise palely like white mice against a green background. A row of green-uniformed policemen stand close behind them. Wanja and Anni are cuffed together, and both of them are cuffed in turn to the green men. They have shackled my childhood, they have put the foolish dream of my childhood in handcuffs: two things are coming together, two things click to that will always seem separate to the outside. There sits my devil, there sits my bit of madness, and he has stopped moving. They have caught him, and I stand on the side of the free ones, the victors, I am one of them, I wear their uniform and their imperial insignia. I have always been so fearful and clever and cautious, and now I feel a bit pitiful.

My God, I have always lacked your strength and your madness, Wanja. You said no and I said yes. The world has gone mad. Yes or no, now we're all tangled up in this. Some people kill and others are killed, some people judge and others are judged. It's turned into a confused and terrible world: yes or no, no or yes. We're all in it now. The world is divided into two camps; in this world now there are only the persecutors and the persecuted. Yes or no, we're all trapped in it.

How do I continue with this story? Where do I start now? The stories written by life are hard to tell. They're so direct. Right now I should be telling the story of how I came home from Prague, how I returned to Frankfurt with nothing but that name in my head. It was a conjecture and a bit more than that, and it wouldn't leave me in peace. I thought: A name, what does that mean, a name, read in a newspaper in Prague after twenty years, there are so many names in this world, a name needn't mean anything. And then I thought again: Perhaps, it could be, it might just by chance actually be him. Who knows in this crazy world? The name wouldn't leave me in peace. So one day I wrote to *Neues Deutschland*, I asked whether its Middle East correspondent from Cairo might be

Wanja. It could be, if you bear in mind how life plays out. And after four or five weeks I actually received a reply from East Berlin, and *Neues Deutschland* informed me on official grey paper that it was him, it was actually him, if my data were correct. They would check. And later – after checking – they wrote that unfortunately they couldn't tell me his address in Cairo, because their correspondents were always on the move, but I could write directly to *Neues Deutschland* or even better I could go and see them; old anti-fascists were always welcome at their address.

Then there was a lot of back and forth that lasted more than six months. Things had been resolved in the meantime, and Wanja had vouched for me to his paper. After a lengthy pause, they wrote just before Christmas to tell me to come, because he was going to be coming too. In fact, between Christmas Eve and New Year *Neues Deutschland* always organises a big meeting of correspondents. At this event the people's correspondents are presented to the people and have to account for themselves in Dresden and Weimar and Rostock. It's socialism's idea of a party, a present from *Neues Deutschland* to the people and its correspondents – and it would also be of benefit to me.

So I met up with Wanja. It was Christmas 1964. It was a touching and painful reunion – I should never have done it. We can't catch up with our dreams. We didn't meet at the offices of *Neues Deutschland*; that was just too stiff and official for the Christmas season. I met him at the Press Café at Friedrichstrasse station, where those visitors from the West who take themselves intellectually seriously sometimes stop off. It's a sort of centre of the intelligentsia, or of cultural workers, as they say there; I have never quite understood the language of progress.

For quite a while I sat alone at a small table that reminded me of Café Kranzler or Zuntz in the 1930s. The tables here are all heavy glass and stiff wood like everything cosy in Prussia in the 1930s; even the menus are behind glass, tall-stemmed and with a heavy silver coating at the bottom, and promise old delights at 1930s prices. It's all very respectable.

I had ordered tea with a bit of lemon. They told me you couldn't have lemon with tea, and they said it as if I'd made an improper request. Later a woman joined me at my table, an old lady with the face of a north German grandmother who had seen better days. The old lady started drinking coffee with a lot of elegant and extravagant gestures, and because she had clearly also asked an impertinent question, she was informed that there was no cream, but there was no shortage of condensed milk in the German Democratic Republic. All of these things are banal, admittedly, and they shouldn't really be worth mentioning by someone who's been through all these things with Wanja and Hitler and the People's Court. It's just that I'm appalled by the tone in which they speak. In the New Germany they always feel immediately provoked, and have a very pointed and categorical way of delivering a rebuke, which they think goes back to Karl Marx but only ever reminds me of frustrated women: nuns in hospitals or English governesses. They always want to instruct and reprimand you. I don't like it.

After a while the old lady, who could probably tell by looking at me that I came from the West, struck up a conversation. She looked at me probingly. Of course the conversation began with cream and moved from there to condensed milk and from condensed milk to sugar, tangible things that old women know more about than people like us do. She praised the sugar because it came from Cuba, but she was certain that our sugar in the West was better – everything we had was better, after all.

As she spoke she looked at me quizzically, suspiciously and expectantly, and was properly disappointed when I said no, not everything we had was better, you couldn't see it that way either. Then she slowly started telling a story, getting lost in her own memories; it was like a long-submerged past that she had brought with her from a village somewhere near Rostock. It was about storing potatoes for the winter, and how they had taken her three hundredweight back out of the cellar even though everything had been quite officially distributed and had been lying nice and dark in the cellar. And generally speaking, how they treated them: herring and twenty-five grams of butter on food cards these days. Well, all right, she added after a pause, as if soothing herself, Berlin on the other hand was something like a paradise, one would have to say.

And while the woman went off again and really started to blossom, having found somebody on the second day of the Christmas holidays in the Press Café on Friedrichstrasse who would listen to all her stories like quaint sagas from a far-off land and who only shook his head every now and again – in walked Wanja. I recognised him immediately by his stocky frame and the liver stain on his neck, and I was startled. I was suddenly afraid that our reunion was an act of madness. For a second I think: No, it can't be, it's wrong, it's impossible, it's just impossible for us to act as if there are only twenty-three years between us – there are centuries between us. How are you supposed to bridge centuries?

But there's no stopping it, he must have recognised me too, Wanja was always so sure of himself. He steers right towards me. The woman beside me suddenly has her mouth wide open, and looks up at us, a bit frightened and perplexed. I have got to my feet and now we're shaking hands like old pals and we are laughing and we attempt a rather helpless and embarrassing hug with a fraternal kiss of the kind familiar from official socialist receptions. These are more or less the tried-and-tested gestures of reunion, the sign language of the body that is supposed to help you over the first few tongue-tied seconds.

How are you supposed to start, what are you supposed to say, and what's the first important thing? What's supposed to be the most important thing after twenty-three years? And you usually get it wrong, you get stuck on something trivial, you say something quite banal, something about your cloak-room ticket, about the weather outside or the waiter that you're about to call over. Just embarrassments, just excuses. You're better off starting with the physical appearance and saying: You've barely changed, Wanja, and thinking: Actually he was different. You say: I recognised you at the door, Wanja, and you think: What's up with him? He looks so upright and bourgeois. The mystery has gone from him. You say: You've turned out fabulously, Wanja, and think: What's up with him? The madness is gone. He's wearing a boring grey suit, his hair is neatly parted, and the back of his neck isn't furry any more. Now he sits on tall chairs like everyone else. He looks like just anybody, except he wears a lot of badges on his jacket, silver, red and mottled badges that mean nothing to me. 'So how are you these days?' I ask, suddenly tormented. It's quite a dreadful question after twenty-three years of Hitler and Ulbricht,* which can only prompt a similarly dreadful answer. Wanja says: 'Very good, dear friend. We're all very well here, as you can see. What about you?'

Luckily we soon agreed to leave the café. Everything in there was so cramped and stiff and heavy, it was just impossible. Outside it had started snowing. Friedrichstrasse lay white and empty in front of us. A few old-fashioned cars hummed towards Unter den Linden. In front of a low building there was a banner inviting people to an art exhibition from Inner Mongolia. A distant, foreign, cold world. A sharp wind blew over the Spree. 'Remember when we used to walk around here, Wanja?' I say. 'God, there used to be a bustling city centre here, on Friedrichstrasse and around the station: full of little racketeers and pimps, full of girls and rent boys, and on every square metre a stall – ties, ladies' underwear, gemstones, bookies and sausage stands. It was a busy place around here, do you remember?' Wanja barely seems to be listening. He just shrugs, pushes a bit of snow around in front of him with his shoes and says nothing. We walked along Dorotheenstrasse to the university, past the state library. It was an embarrassed and aimless walk – where to? We were looking for a way back.

'Now tell me,' I said. 'What?' he says. 'What do you want me to tell you?' 'What happened to you back then?' 'What do you mean, back then?' 'Well, back then when you were up before the People's Court; I wasn't allowed to be there when sentence was passed.'

Wanja waves dismissively and shrugs again. Then he says: 'Five years.' 'Hm,' I say. 'That's a lot. Five years of what?' 'P,' he says, just P, and I remember that in prisoner language that meant prison. So he'd been in prison, and now he was slowly starting to remember, he was slowly starting to tell his story; it was quite a terrible story of our time. He had been given five years' imprisonment for high treason, and Anni Korn fifteen. No, it hadn't been all that bad. In those days people had been very keen on long prison sentences because as long as you were in the hands of the law you were safe from the concentration camp. That had saved both their lives. They had been liberated by the Red Army in 1945 and immediately became involved in the reconstruction. And then they had both studied social sciences in Leipzig, had got married and later joined the staff of *Neues Deutschland*. And for two years now he had had the honour of representing his paper in Cairo. He really said 'the honour'.

So Wanja had become a communist. I say that without any undertones of suspicion, revulsion or that arrogant demonisation attached to the word in the West today. I'm just saying how it was. He had fallen out of Hitler's empire and into the empire of the Soviets. For him the Red Army had been the liberator, the Party the good, late teacher. It must have been something like an education through German history: first Westfälische Strasse, then Hitler, then prison and then the new beginning with the Russians – the Red Army as father and the Party as mother. He had never had a real parental home. Now he swore by those who had taken him under their wing: so Wanja had become a son of the Soviets. In 1947 he had joined the SED, the East German Communist Party, and now had a truth that he defended with eager zealousness. He was a committed Marxist. It was the only way to ease the burden of his youth. He wanted to survive and he had chosen the simplest, clearest way to do so: the new state was his family home; he was devoted to it. Now he was the one under a spell, and I could no longer follow him.

During those Christmas days we got together twice more in East Berlin. Our attempts were in vain; things became more and more difficult between us. Basically we had nothing more to say to each other. It wasn't his new faith: you can have wonderful arguments with real Marxists. It was the banal and spell-like devotion of his faith, where everything was so flat; it was that limited and narrow-minded socialism, which felt clumsy and unreflective as if he was reading out official slogans. It was this put-on and cramped communism that fitted precisely with this cramped New Germany. Wanja was simply a spokesman for agitation and propaganda, and he substituted loyalty for reason and enthusiasm for arguments. He said: 'The Red Flag is on the moon!' And I said: 'That's great, Wanja, but there are a few things that need doing in East Berlin too. The houses are pretty shabby – after twenty years.' He wasn't listening but said: 'You know what that means? The moon has become a Soviet planet. The stars revolve around Communism.' And then later he talked about imperialism and revanchism, of head-hunters and spy swamps and why didn't I come over to them; they were the Germany of the future.

What he was saying was pretty awful, everything was as flat as if it came from the radio, so I stayed silent. I stayed increasingly silent. It wasn't until we were downstairs in Friedrichstrasse station, and I was full of sadness, and he said: 'Believe me: socialism will win!', that I replied with a hint of irony, and fully aware of what I was saying: 'Fine, Wanja, then you go right ahead and win' – and I never saw him again.

Time, time, the way it colours things, yellows, darkens and slowly submerges them: Herr Focken and Walter Flex, your balalaika and all the letters – even the woman in the Press Café is almost forgotten. Time heals all wounds, they say. But is that really true? Doesn't it open up new wounds that never heal? It only covers everything up as a mother covers things up with her apron, and one day we have grown up, our mother is gone, the apron has been taken off and everything is there again: on a huge scale. My God, I'm no longer a child looking for miracles. My God, I'm no longer an adolescent in love with madness. The time of Hölderlin and Nietzsche in Eichkamp is over. Now I'm a man with his memories, his eccentricities, his arrogance, his hip flask of whisky and his late-life neuroses, and I can't understand that this is what had to happen to us.

Wanja, it's over between us – of course. It's over for ever. I ask you: What made us such strangers to each other? What was it? We once studied the same grammar at the same desk in Berlin. I think it's just the times. Wanja, these crazy, megalomaniac times that devoured us and vomited us up again and spat us out on foreign shores. Now we both smell quite revoltingly of the times: you of the East and I of the West. Time has just spat us both out like that. We were sired by beaten, clueless fathers, and our mothers were awkward and loveless. Things like that stick to you, they go with you, they themselves become a kind of fate. My youth was cluelessness, emptiness, awkwardness, and yours was a crazy, short dream. They just didn't give us anything that would stand up to time: it was all nothing but dreams and illusions; we were easy prey for the times.

Wanja, we're a botched generation. We didn't have a real family home. So you chose the Party as your mother and the Red Army as your father, and I have nothing at all but my memories, my irony and my middle-aged neuroses. I sit here in Frankfurt and write for the West – naturally. And you sit in Cairo and write for the East – naturally. Is it really natural? It's a dreadful story: a really trashy tale and romance of the divided Germany – pan-German waffle. You can't serve that up to anybody any more. Why does life write such bad stories? Two schoolboys from Berlin who once stood together against Herr Focken and against Hitler and were then, like Germany, torn apart in the Great German War – they couldn't find each other again.

There's nothing I like better than Erbsenbrei – pease pudding. Erbsenbrei is my favourite food. You can serve it with bacon, with dried meat, with brawn or simply with Frankfurters – it's always dependable: an honest German dish that gives the stomach the feeling of having had something solid, tangibly conveyed. It makes the whole body feel warm and firm. A little more liquid and it's called Erbsensuppe, and is still worth a trip to Aschinger. Even back then it was a Berlin speciality: Erbsensuppe with bacon and plenty of small bread rolls that cost forty-five pfennigs, and even as a stew it counted as an honest German dish. A bit firmer and it's called Erbsenpurée, and is ideal with onions and sauerkraut for cold winter days.

It wasn't a cold winter day, it was December and I was eating Erbsenbrei; I was making my body warm and firm with that honest dish. I was sitting in our dining room at that heavy, rectangular table that had been modestly pushed together again since Ursula's funeral. It was a day like any other: Friday evening, just before eight. That afternoon I had had a university seminar on Plato; the relationship between the true and the beautiful had been discussed in Socratic terms. I had already been studying philosophy for two semesters on Unter den Linden. Lately I had heard a lot about antinomies and aporias, and not only in Plato. My parents wouldn't have understood; but they had kept my dinner warm in the oven.

It had been cold at Friedrichstrasse station, draughty and cold. I was frozen. Berlin was very dark and cold at the time. The lights of the big city had gone out months before; it was wartime. But at home we noticed little of that. I was eating my peas with bacon, warm from the oven. The dish was steaming, thick and hot in front of me. It was greyish yellow and tasted slightly of the oven, and our black grandfather clock was striking eight. My parents were sitting in the next room, discussing Christmas matters in the study. It was to be our first wartime Christmas. Merry Christmas during Germany's defensive struggle – there was much food for thought.

Suddenly our doorbell rang. It was unusual to hear our doorbell at that time of day. Eight o'clock in our house was already very late and bedtime wasn't far off. 'I'll get it!' my father called brightly from the next room, indicating that he wanted to take full charge of the unusual situation. I heard him walking down the corridor, fiddling with the keyring, opening our security lock and talking to somebody outside. My head is full of Plato, my palate completely full of pease pudding, when I suddenly hear my father uttering a muted cry. He comes down the corridor and throws open the dining-room door. Now he's displaying a big and frightened face, those troubled childish eyes that all civil servants have, he stands trembling and quizzing in front of me and doesn't say a word, he just speaks with those eyes: a man in distress.

And like a worker in a canteen I set the spoon down on the table and slowly rise to my feet; I'm lanky and I've grown much too tall for this house and I think: What can be happening at eight o'clock on an evening in Advent, when you're having your dinner? I walk down the corridor and suddenly I see Franz Bradtke standing in our front door. White snowy air swirls in from the darkness outside. Herr Bradtke stands stiffly to attention like a green tin soldier in our doorway. I've known him since childhood. He's a calm, lumbering man with a brown moustache, a real village policeman that a child could look up to as if he was God the Father. But now Herr Bradtke is officially wearing the tall, gleaming helmet of all uniformed Berlin policemen, with the strap pulled over his chin. He exudes importance, he is visibly on duty. Beside him, a light brown Alsatian wheezes on a thick leather leash. They both stand there larger than life and glittering with snow in our front doorway like terrifying figures from a fairy tale; they almost threaten to turn our house upside down. And I hear Herr Bradtke, who was still speaking to me in familiar terms only a few years ago, you little rogue and so on, suddenly rasping in a strangely altered voice: 'You, come with me!' And when I just stare at him, he repeats very officially, and very formally: 'Right, come with me, young man!' He said nothing more after that. And that was the beginning of the end of our Eichkamp family, that's how quickly a family, that indestructible foundation of our moral world order, can fall apart. On that Friday evening in 1939 a German family was undone, a family that had fought stubbornly and doggedly against everything destructive and corrosive in our country since 1914, since the day war broke out on the first of August. They were taking the last child away. The house was empty. And while I looked, helpless and astonished, at Herr Bradtke, and heard my mother calling from the study: 'What's going on? I'm not here!' I knew immediately: You've got to go with him.

I went back into the corridor, grabbed my coat, looked for my gloves and a handkerchief because my mouth was still full of Erbsenbrei, and thought: Dear parents! So it's come to this. They're coming to get me. Your dreams are over, the time of beautiful lies is past. Your son is going away now. I know you didn't deserve this. I would have liked to become what you hoped I would: a civil servant, perhaps, an upright German citizen, the kind with children and a pretty wife and a proper office in the city that you can see. You would have deserved that. But it's not what happened; I'm different. That's how life is. That's how family dies, that's how it must perish. I'm coming along.

Even before my father had quite grasped the situation I was outside and had slammed the door behind me. Was this the pull of the outside world? Snow whirled in the street, and all kinds of confused thoughts whirled through my head. There was fear inside me, but something else as well: an absurd and bizarre feeling of salvation. That's how you go away! That's what it's like when boys leave their parents. Walking in the snow in Eichkamp is very pleasant. There are hardly any cars here, the pines of the Grunewald loom into the sky, tall and black: wintry peace in Prussia. You walk softly and silently as if over white carpets, and even police boots sound different here. It was already the third week of Advent, and the houses were surrounded by the peace of Christmas. We didn't meet anyone coming in the opposite direction. Only once did we see a woman, carrying a little Christmas tree under her arm. Herr Bradtke's boots crunched in the snow and gave our walk an official tone. His steps were those of a man on a mission. He said nothing, and even the panting of his Alsatian was silent on our way to the station.

Police stations in Germany always smell of cold smoke and leather, of the sweat of little people with a hint of turpentine. They are painted grey, they are cold, they have yellow wooden barriers, wooden benches and office chairs, and there is always a portrait of a man hanging on the wall; in those days it was a picture of our Führer. And behind the barriers there are always lists and forms to be filled in. Herr Bradtke worked on a document and sometimes looked up expectantly when a car could be heard on the main road, then calmed the dog whose ears had pricked up, went on writing, looked up again and shook his head once. He had put his helmet in front of him beside the inkwell. Now he was an official compiling a report; he passed a report on to the senior officials and was doubtless writing in gothic script with long high loops at the top and emphatic downward strokes. After each line he dipped the steel pen into the black inkwell. One can sense the effort that goes into such a report destined for the authorities higher up. It is as if everything in the office is creaking: the policeman's boots creak, his joints, the fibrous wooden floor, and something in his brain is bound to be creaking too as the pen scratches over the paper. Herr Bradke doesn't say a word, but his breathing is audible. It is a heavy, rattling breath, a real policeman's breath, that has been made very noticeable by age and tobacco and the weight of office. You can hear what's happening inside the men's chests; nothing is hidden. Presumably that's how it's supposed to be.

No one turned up until eleven. Then I heard doors slamming and men's footsteps, and two policemen came in, saluted and said 'Heil Hitler' with a laugh. They brought a lot of snow in with them, and then I was taken to the prisoners' van that they call Green Minna in Berlin. From outside it really is green, it has no windows and is sealed, but inside there's a window to the driver's seat, and running around the iron walls are iron benches that you can sit on. I was all by myself and could feel nothing but iron. And then the vehicle set off. It was probably just beginning its round out here, then it criss-crossed Berlin, drove from police station to police station and picked up whoever needed picking up that evening. A motley little collection came together. In Charlottenburg – I heard the name being called – two lads were taken on board who looked dangerous and had filthy bandages around their heads. They grinned from narrow slits of eyes and searched their coat pockets for threads of leftover tobacco. At Zoo three girls were brought in. They wore fur coats and little lambskin boots and looked very elegant. They had lurid make-up and they wanted to smoke as well. They swore loudly, giggled and said to me: 'Hey, Lanky, got a fag?' and roared with laughter again. Then came three old men who didn't say a thing, and then another boy in a suede jacket, and an old woman who talked loudly to herself and hissed: 'I'll show them!' On Friedrichstrasse a handsome young man was pushed into the vehicle; the girls immediately addressed him as Fanny and seemed to know him well. Two members of the Hitler Youth later staggered in, cuffed together at the wrist. They maintained a defiant silence.

By midnight the van was full. It smelled of beer and make-up, of tobacco and sweat. They were a wild bunch, and they sometimes flew squealing in all directions when the van braked suddenly. Here the debris of a big city was collected, a vehicle full of debris, of the kind that is found in every city. I was sitting among them thinking: So this is debris being driven around, nothing but Berlin debris.

When the van suddenly came to a standstill after taking many rumbling bends, one of the girls said snippily: 'Moabit, all passengers please alight!' Everybody laughed, the doors were unbolted and the little crowd jumped cheerfully out – they seemed almost at home here. The old woman now swore at the boys with the bandages and gave a shove to the handsome youth, who was acting as indifferently as if this cargo had nothing to do with him. The girls from Zoo trotted carefully along and addressed the police outside by their first names. Here in the courtyard it was dark and wet; everyone was sent to their destinations, and when one of the cops was about to send me along with them I suddenly heard an officer, holding a list in his hand, tell him in a friendly growl: 'Nah, not him, Karle. He's a political. Over to the Gestapo!'

Block 5, cell 103: there's a lot to learn. At half past five a shrill whistle echoes down the corridors and staircases. Seven warders stand on seven floors and start the deafening whistling concert. They blow on these shrill whistles that have summoned generations of Germans to a hero's death, to battle, to interrogation; they call it the big wake-up. After that a dark roar begins; bearded men's voices roar loud, dark, snorting noises. High boots strike concrete floors, keys rattle, iron doors are pulled open and thrown shut again, iron strikes constantly against iron, and someone nearby yells: 'You swine!' – he's probably been caught still on his plank bed – and rattling keys are heard around the building again.

It only takes a few minutes; then everything goes quiet once more. We have woken from our dreams, from dark memories, from other times. I was still in a blue meadow in the Harz mountains, reading *Hyperion*. Even at school I knew it by heart: 'Every morning now I am on the heights of the Corinthian Isthmus, and like bees among flowers my soul often flies back and forth between the seas that cool the feet of my glowing mountains to right and left.' And I go on reciting in the Harz, I go on reciting in Moabit: 'But what does that mean to me? The cry of the jackal, singing its wild dirge beneath antiquity's pile of stones, wakes me from my dreams. Blessed is he who is delighted and strengthened by a flourishing fatherland.'

Now the day is growing. Now the whole of Moabit is washing itself. The little grey enamel bowl into which you can pour water from a tall iron jug has already washed the dirt from generations of prisoners – it will cleanse me too today. It doesn't last long. There is the sound of tubs and heavy iron pots being dragged along the corridors. The invisible, low power of the trusties approaches. They are like insects who have taken up home and spread throughout the building; they have power. That invisible, low army of insects comes closer and closer, we hear them pulling and knocking and rattling, soon the brown cell door will be thrown harshly open, and there are two or three men standing beside the chief warder. They look smooth and pale and thin, like young fish, and they wear the striped blue overalls of apprentice butchers. You hold out a brown enamel cup, and with a long-handled ladle they tip the black stuff into it – you can also have dry bread.

The interrogations start at eight. At first you're not aware of them, you only find out later. All you hear is the key duty that invisible men are now beginning with rattling zeal. Footsteps, shouts, doors being slammed, a word of command, a whistle, then footsteps again, fading away, and then it's quiet. Curiously, every new beginner hopes for an interrogation. Everyone hopes the footsteps will be for him, that they're approaching him, that they will stop outside his door, that one of them will blink through the hatch and then turn the lock to fetch him. It is a foolish and absurd hope. It lives on the slightest sound.

At nine o'clock the sun slowly rises. It is a radiant blue winter day today. The barred window hatch at the top shows only a narrow strip of blue. From time to time they put the heating on, there are clicks and ticks for a while in the realm of the lower pipes, warmth streams in; they are very good at heating in Prussia. Now it's time for our walk. Now everyone in Moabit is going for a walk. Thousands of lonely walkers take the five steps there and back that is all the prison cells allow. It is the time of morning fantasies, of confused hopes and dreams, the round trip of great plans and schemes, that comes and goes like the footsteps outside. You're ready, you have a plan, but it doesn't last for long, it slips away again like glasses on a tray held at an angle. Beneath it lies helplessness, and fear rises up and moves for a while from the heart via the left arm to the head. Then, all of a sudden, you suddenly hear keys rattling outside, and for a moment they bring hope, before it is soon crushed again. What now? Cell walkers are like lost mountaineers: you keep going up and down, there are peaks and crevasses; at the end you're back where you started.

At ten o'clock the sun has advanced so far into the room that the walls begin to talk. All the prison walls in the world tell unimaginable stories; they are the blackboards of the mute. That is where they have scratched their hopes and fears with spoon handles. Like graffiti in public toilets, these phantasmagorias from deep down are obscene – and they reflect the times. 'To hell with Hitler', someone has scratched quite deeply at the bottom, with a naked woman sketched beside it. The words 'Heil Moscow' appear three times in a circular ribbon around a hammer-and-sickle sign right under the woman. Someone has tried to scratch it out and drawn a cross above it: '*Ora pro nobis*', it says. And all the prisoners also keep a calendar. There are always six little lines that stand closely side by side like blades of grass, then one big line, Sunday; and when the week is over, a horizontal line is drawn through the whole thing, and the first of a new little set of blades begins. Here you can read how long everyone had stayed here, because suddenly one of these sets breaks off and doesn't make it to the end of the week.

Food always arrives at one o'clock. Why does lunch always taste so much of prison? How do they do that? 'There's salicylic acid in it,' they said. 'It suppresses the sex drive,' I was told with a laugh. But there's probably also sweat and fear and poverty in it – you can taste the Prussian administration. There are usually peas, a healthy German dish that they have horribly spoiled: peas in potato water, peas in sauerkraut water or just peas on their own. On Sunday a piece of meat is added, which the young butchers swiftly throw in with their masturbators' fists, and which tastes not of meat, but of prison meat, guilty meat. 'They spoil everything here with their salicylic acid,' I was told with a laugh. 'You have to get used to it.' All flesh here is guilty.

At three o'clock in the afternoon the building begins to move again. The business with the keys starts again. Again names are called, people are led past, gangs assembled for work. Keys rattle through the building. Your neighbour has been selected, a stroke of luck, they've just fetched him, and when the three of them walked past you, he gave off the smell of wonderful liberation. Why are they fetching him? Why not me? There are so many mysteries in a prison. They cannot be solved.

Five o'clock in the afternoon: now Moabit is very busy. Now the enemies of state are being interrogated, questioned, heard and confronted with other enemies of state: say that again, admit it, we've known for ages. Now lists are written and minutes taken. I joined the association of pacifists at twenty-nine, yes, I was filled with hatred, I was in the

Communist Party, I had Jews in my business, I was always in favour of Ebert, but I am loyal to the new state. My son is in the Hitler Youth, I didn't want him to join. I don't know anything. These words go whirring through the building now, things are confessed and kept silent, noted and laughingly dismissed: Jesus, are we supposed to believe that? Human beings aren't heroes, only ever in retrospect. They want to live. Human beings are bundles of hope and fear. They lie, of course they lie: 'Oh, human beings are gods when they dream, beggars when they reflect, and once the enthusiasm is gone they stand there like a misbegotten son that the Father has expelled from heaven, studying the few miserable pfennigs that pity gave him for the journey.'

Evening comes quickly and slips swiftly into night. Why do we always sleep so well in prison? The night is dense and black – it doesn't let the police take it prisoner. It comes silently from outside, penetrating all the walls. It comes like a mother, like a woman, and lies spread over the world; like something obscene, opening on to the void. It pulls us along, it sucks at us, we come, we fall, we are submerged. Night is the great oblivion. There is still the sound of keys, of iron and heavy footsteps, sometimes a cry in the next building, but it fades, it moves away, grows quiet, seeps and sinks, becoming dreamlike and unreal. By nine o'clock Moabit has become an anxious dream that lies behind me. I'm free again, I'm outside, I'm dreaming. Night cannot be thrown in chains.

Sleep is the freedom of all prisoners. They let us have it. That's what they leave us with. We are able to forget. I will dream of wonderful worlds, of a blue meadow in the Harz mountains, and will read *Hyperion* again: 'Like the worker in refreshing sleep, my disputed essence sinks often into the arms of the innocent past. The peace of childhood! Heavenly peace! How often do I stand silently before you in loving contemplation, trying to fathom you!'

So suddenly I found myself trapped between the millstones of history and I barely understood how I had got there. Overnight I had become an enemy of the state, and I was very unsuited to the role. I had only sat with Wanja in the evenings, I had distributed those letters and was now caught up in the worst thing that had ever happened to me. I will never forget it. I only learned of it slowly. The crime was called high treason, and it stretched like a subterranean sickness across the whole country. The charge was 'preparation for high treason against the writer Broghammer and others', and those others were a hundred and one people who had all been arrested that night. I didn't know them. I knew only Wanja, who was a little appendage of Anni Korn, who had in turn been a little appendage of somebody else, and that person had in turn been appended to that one, and that one to someone else – those are the classic rules of conspiracy. You have to work like that in the underground. Now they were all sitting here being interrogated one by one.

I was often interrogated too, at least at the start. They didn't beat me or stick me in cold water like others. They didn't put me in dark solitary confinement, they didn't pull my arm out of its socket as they did with others. During the interrogation they sat opposite me, quite smart and attentive, their names were Müller and Dr Stein and Krause, typical German names, they smoked cigarettes and said please and thank you and 'Herr' and 'Sie',* and they had probably soon noticed that they hadn't really got anything on me, or nothing on which anything political could be built. In a safe they kept a fat file on me that surprised me and at the same time unexpectedly exonerated me. They had checked my post for almost a year, they had opened and photocopied all the letters I had received, and then sealed them again and sent them to me. I had never noticed a thing. These letters, which now lay photocopied on the left-hand page of the file, with typewritten extracts on the right, were my salvation. What sort of letters are written by a nineteen-year-old boy from Eichkamp, a son of apolitical parents, a son of the bourgeoisie, a philosophy student with a weakness for Hölderlin and Nietzsche, and what sort of letters does he receive? They were rather extravagant and crazy letters, letters of friendship, epistles of grief and hymns of enthusiasm, messages of loneliness and celebrations of the soul – O Bellarmin, O Hyperion – stammering and hastily flung together. It was the typical adolescent bourgeois waffle of a nineteen-year-old at the time. None of it was played out down in the stalls of world history, it was all suspended very high up, it hung like sparkling sequins of the soul, high up in the flies of German inspiration, it was readings of Schiller and Fichte, it was lofty Novalis and Wackenroder, it was attempts to engage emotionally with Rilke and Hesse – it was quite embarrassing and adolescent.* But political it wasn't.

It was all very German and inward-looking and made me look like the searcher and the idealist who had made one foolish misstep. I must have looked like a terrible muddle-head, a real German youth with his head full of beauty, death and madness, and somewhere they had a trace of respect for that. It wasn't completely alien to them, just a little too elevated. They soon registered me on the side of the victims, the dreamers and idealists. I was a victim of the counter-revolution, a victim of Wanja and his girlfriend Anni. That was what Herr Krause said to me one evening after a long interrogation session, and clapped me on the shoulder.

I didn't contradict him, ever. I thought: So you might be able to get out of it. And thought: It's actually true, too. We were always apolitical at home.

After three months they transferred me to another block. I was put in a shared cell; they probably intended that as a form of relief. This configuration was very new to me. Coming from Eichkamp I now found myself entirely surrounded by politicals. There was no one from Eichkamp in Moabit. There were only Communists, trade unionists and other Reds who had rebelled. There were Poles and other enemies of the Reich, there were Czechs and other enemies of the Protectorate, there were Jews, the spouses of Jews, the servants of Jews and other enemies of the state. Radio criminals who had secretly listened to Strasbourg or Basel and blabbed about it, currency criminals who had taken Reichsmarks abroad, economic criminals who had bought a quarter pound of sausage without a ration card and thus undermined the war economy. Then there were the boycotters, the carpers and intellectuals who had broken the Treachery Act by making disparaging comments, malicious joke-tellers with a subversive edge, and others who were just enemies of the Reich. The whole world at the time was full of enemies, full of Untermenschen,* saboteurs and bloodsuckers who wanted to undermine our poor, proud land. I got to know them here in Moabit.

And I got to know prison, the world of prisoners, the language of detention, the rituals of hope and resignation, prisoners' rituals: kneading chessmen out of bread, smoking so that no one could smell it, giving knocking signals, sending secret messages, making playing cards out of old paper bags, the joys of corridor duty, picking up information while shaving, talking during exercise in the yard without moving one's lips. It's a pitiful and refined art, the language of prisoners, it lives on signs on doors and walls, it lives on the faintest sounds, it scrabbles together scraps of tobacco and straw, it spends ages listening at cell doors, it learns how to distinguish the most delicate differences in tone and it falls for a while upon every new arrival, it squeezes him dry as if he carried the secrets of the world beneath his jacket. Tell us, what's going on? Come on, tell us, what's happening out there? Every newcomer is a hope that flares up, survives for a while and then seeps slowly away again into dull brooding. The newcomer is from another block. He's been here for almost a year and has the mischievous face of a little crook. He demands cigarette-ends in return for outlandish rumours: We're being transferred, you'll see, a commission will be here tomorrow, from April there's going to be something to smoke, there was a health inspection in C-block yesterday, next week the old ones are going to be sent over to Tegel, the politicals will be going to Prinz Albrecht Strasse, the rest will be off to work at Siemens and so on. It spills through the cracks in the doors and keyholes, spreads in a flash down the corridors and into other cells, it clings rigidly to the wall for a while, then flakes away to the floor and dissolves again. Rumours are the prisoners' daily newspapers.

Friday is always the change of shift in Moabit. The most stubborn prisoners are taken out and sent off to be softened up. Two o'clock is corridor inspection: everyone out, line up, stand still, attention. The cell elder reports to the Kapo, the Kapo to the door-locker, the door-locker to the senior warder and he to the inspector. After a while some gentlemen come, senior officials it seems, in elegant suits, the commissars of the secret service, and have lists read out to them. They don't do it themselves. They just stand there. They stand to the side and sometimes grin when a familiar name is mentioned: Bethke, Karl – step forward. You see, Bethke, you could have spared yourself all this, couldn't you? Did Bethke know that? They have their methods here, they don't get their hands dirty. Men who don't come up with the goods even though they have something to tell, as has Bethke, for example, are moved for six weeks to Oranienburg for special treatment by the SS. They are kneaded until they are soft. Then we'll see.

At six in the evening the cars come back bringing the people from six weeks ago: Bunsen, Hermann; Meister, Kurt; Schuhmacher, Horst; Levi, Siegfried, who was so quiet and was therefore kneaded for six weeks to make him nice and helpful. Berlin-Moabit is almost a convalescence, everybody longs to be here. Now he'll talk: he'll say everything.

It's dark in the cell. It's a gloomy March day and almost night by six, there are occasional flakes of snow outside, when Levi, Siegfried is delivered to us. A thin brownish light burns over the cell door. I see the little man stumble in, see him stand fearful and helpless by the wooden bunks and hear him asking in a polite voice: 'Where may I sit, gentlemen?' Silence, laughter, snorting in the room – have they ever heard anything like this before? Gentlemen? He lay next to me at night and kept asking over and over: 'Do they beat you here as well – with those bulls' pizzles?' And I said after a pause: 'No, not that I know of', and then I pass him some bread, an old dried-up end that I still had under my pillow. 'Eat something,' I say quietly, 'Christ, you must be half starving!' Then after a while Levi, Siegfried started whimpering, he took deep breaths, he suddenly started panting anxiously, the panting soon turned into sobs, and then off he went. The little bald man, who had previously owned a jewellery shop below the Bülowbogen, and who had always been a gentleman, even in Oranienburg, burst into loud childish wails, he sobbed and groaned away: 'Now they're going to come and beat me again, you can't eat out of turn, sir, don't you know that?' It was ridiculous: he was very funny, the strange Herr Levi. In spite of everything he often made us laugh.

One day my parents are there. It's both terrible and wonderful to receive such news in Moabit. It makes me quite ill. They fetch me from the cell, they lead me down long, iron corridors, there are three spiral staircases down, then down more corridors, still made of iron. Then comes a big-barred cell, a proper cage, that they push me into, papers are signed, and a man in plain clothes takes charge of me and leads me back down lots of corridors, this time with wooden doors and linoleum floors. There is a smell of turpentine. My gait is quite stiff and rigid, I hold my shoulders hunched like a marionette and my hands clenched behind my back, and act as if none of it has anything to do with me, and think: Your parents are here – haven't you heard? How did they manage to come to your jail? How did they get in here?

The man in plain clothes didn't take me to a visitor cell, he took me to his office. My parents were of the better sort, and there they sat. I gave a start. They had come a long way. They sat on high chairs: anxious, touching, and somehow distraught – with love. They looked so elegant. My mother wore a shiny fur coat, a silky dress, and pearls around her neck. She always wore those to the opera. She had opened a cardboard suitcase on the floor. As always, she had thought wonderfully of everything, she had brought socks and underpants and a white nightshirt, and now she stumbled over and lay in my arms and kept crying out: 'My son, my poor son,' and then started weeping properly like in an opera. They have brought my suitcase from Eichkamp, all those little things from before: shaving things and handkerchiefs, a towel and also some writing materials, a lot of warm socks, and *Hyperion* is there as well; I recognise them all as mine.

And I would like to write them a letter: It was really nice of you to visit me. Thank you for all the lovely things. I'm sure they won't let me keep them, but still. And all best wishes to you from your son. That's more or less how it would go. But that's not how it works; they're here, they're really here in the room. Now I need to say something. Not everything, just something. How do you do that? My father looks very old and gaunt, he looks at me with the big, anxious childish eyes that all civil servants have and just keeps whispering: The minister, the minister, I talked about your case with the minister. You'll soon be free. And then he gulps, which makes me look away. It's a truly great family scene from the Bible: the lost son, or rather, the lost parents. They find each other again in the end, there's a happy ending – usually. The fatted calf doesn't always have to be slaughtered; love lasts for ever, as it says on so many gravestones. Come back, my son, all is forgiven. You sometimes see that on religious posters around the city.

'Herr Kommissar', I later hear my mother saying. She has turned, pleading, towards the Gestapo officer, with her beautiful, theatrical gestures. She is still an unusual and imposing woman, she has a glamour about her – after all, she did want to join the opera as a singer, and something of that remains. 'Herr Kommissar, our son is innocent!' she says imperiously. 'Believe us, we know him. We have always been apolitical.' And my father has risen to his feet. 'Never,' he says, 'has there been such a thing in our family – high treason. Impossible, in our family.'

My God, it's all so touching and filled with love. They now stand before the officer like two broken angels and plead for their son. My God, they are still dreaming that old family dream, they still believe in the fairy tale that began in 1914, on 1 August, on the day when war broke out, when they got married. They wanted to cover the cracks with love. They wanted to glue over this crack in the world with family: our family, our son, our house. My dears, isn't it all broken and sundered?

It's terrible: at such big moments I feel only rigid and cold, I'm motionless and can't say a word. It's not until I'm alone that life returns to me. I think: Now you'll go home, sad and yet comforted, you will sit on the local train, helpless and mute. You no longer understand your son, who is surrounded by politicals. But we have always been completely apolitical. They will walk through the empty house, the floorboards creak. It's quiet and harsh, and they will go on hoping that everything will turn out well. They are so kind. They are like anxious children lying behind a windowpane waiting for a miracle. Everybody's waiting for a miracle. It's not going to happen. The play is over, we've been through the script, the stage is empty – but you're still wandering about, my dears. Now you're in Eichkamp and I'm in Moabit, you're in that little house and I'm in my cell; that will be the ending, the end of an upright German family.

Then came the night of reckoning. The preliminary investigation by the Gestapo was over. When a case has gone as far as this, we know it is passed on to the investigating judge. He then has to decide, he has to summon every individual prisoner, he has to see whether the evidence to hand is enough to pass to the state prosecution service and press charges. Sometimes you can also be discharged. It's a forensic procedure that they like to stick to. It gives things a legal appearance. Wonderful games can be played with justice.

It was early April, and I was already fast asleep. It was just after midnight. Then they came to get me. They got me out of my bunk and shouted: 'Right, out you come, get on with it, get a move on, lad. Having a nice sleep?' Locks clicked and keys rattled with great haste and authority. Then off we went again down those iron corridors, down basement passageways, through heavy reinforced doors that were awkwardly opened up and then bolted shut again. The policemen's boots rang out loudly on the stone floor. There was a sense of importance in it. I was stiff no longer, the rigidity had gone from me. I thought: Everyone's asleep in Moabit now, but something has happened in your case. Now something's happening, something's going to change.

They led me along a gloomy labyrinth; there was an underground realm here, a dark city within the city, it went on and on, then around another corner, and then suddenly I was standing in a dark corridor and could go no further. I was held by two policemen who stood powerfully beside me. We're standing by a wall, and after a while I recognised other prisoners and other policemen who had also been standing along the wall. My eyes gradually accustomed themselves to the sparse light. I saw a long, gloomy basement corridor, along whose walls prisoners were lined up on both sides. They stood there as if nailed to the spot, and between every two prisoners there was a policeman, an endless chain lost somewhere in the darkness. They had all the defendants in the state vs the writer Broghammer and others. I didn't know them. I was seeing their faces for the first time. I was seeing the other, secret Germany. It looked pale and confused and bizarre; it was a gathering of subterraneans.

Enemies of state look curiously similar to one another. They look pitiful and frightening, they wear ragged suits that are far too big for them, they show cadaverous, bearded faces; a hint of life twitches occasionally in their dead eyes. They are surrounded by darkness. One would hardly believe that these are the heroes of the resistance who are always described to us today as so brave and radiant – that's not how they are. They are more like partisans in war: their clothes torn, starving, with an aura of crime and guilt about them. They are solitary figures and don't have a uniform to protect them. Everyone now bears his own responsibility for what he has done. Everyone carries his own guilt. They may once have been journalists and writers – now they are just criminals. They may once have been students and professors – now they are just remains, victims, their strength broken. They are not going to impress anyone.

The chain moved on very slowly; every now and again it shifted forwards a few metres. Right at the front was a door which, when it was opened, threw out a bright beam of light that enveloped the figure nearest to it, illuminated it brightly for a moment, drew it in, and then the door slammed shut. The corridor was in darkness again. Waiting, standing, silence, then the chain shifts forward again. Slowly I can make out the wall ahead of me again. Now a massive fellow is standing there, with tousled hair and a beard. He looks like a gypsy or a Bohemian professor; he runs his tongue over his lower lip and then bites it. He stands like an ancient tree between the two young and sturdy policemen who flank him like green-clad foresters. They have trapped their prey.

Suddenly bright light floods around me. I'm standing in the investigating judge's office. I stagger slightly, everything here is so hot and bright as day. The room is bare and empty. The only objects are files stacked on a desk. The man behind the files looks old and wrinkled, very small and mouse-grey. He wears a rimless gold pince-nez and keeps looking at the files and then again at me, comparing and checking, and then bends over his desk again and reads and ponders for a while. I am standing very close to his desk, and right in front of me I see two tall piles of papers. They are forms, I can now see, two tall stacks of forms, pre-printed, one green, the other bright red. I turn my head slightly to the side, blink and decipher on the red stack the word COMMITTAL, and the green one clearly says RELEASE. The words are printed in bold black type, each followed by an exclamation mark. Blood suddenly starts throbbing in my throat, the word 'release' is there, it's suddenly there, I never believed it while I've been here, it's there on green paper, big and fat, and now it's throbbing in my throat and dancing around the room and whirling around my head. Now you just have to be quiet and wait, something in me says. He has to reach for a piece of paper, he has to decide between red and green. He has to do that in the end.

Suddenly he started interrogating me. He wanted to know what I thought about Wanja and why and what for and for how long. And I said: 'I've always known him, since fifth form; he was just my friend.' 'The assessment of you isn't bad,' he replies, and points to his files with a pencil. 'You come from a respectable family. How can you choose such friends?' I shrug and say: 'I don't know. It's just how it was.' He sinks into his armchair again and says after a while, without looking up: 'Do you know what ruling our colleagues have made about you?' I say nothing, and he suddenly continues: 'I'll read it out to you: With good treatment, may perhaps still be saved for the völkisch state.' And after a pause, during which he has put the pencil between his lips at an angle and looks at me critically: 'Well, what do you say? Is that true?' I just nod and stare at the two stacks of paper, green and red, and think: Which one is he going to pick? Perhaps green, if treated well? I suddenly feel a paralysing fear within me, the fear that it's going to go on like this for ever here, just interrogations, questionings, cells and locks, you're not going to get out, you're stuck in here, and I see him reaching for the red pile and say quietly: 'Let me out of here, your honour – my God!' Then some time passed, he looked at me with penetrating thoughtfulness, suddenly pushed the files away from him, rose to his feet and leant forward; it was only now that I could see how small he was. He reached with his right hand for one of the stacks, drew a green form towards him, said nothing and just started writing.

I'm free, I'm free, I can hardly believe it. What is that – freedom? A smell, a taste, a hint of world, everything. I breathe in deeply, it's April, there is already a touch of spring in the air. I walk down the streets of the city, I walk as if anaesthetised past shops, past restaurants, past little vegetable carts with green cabbage and oranges, I hear a woman shouting, I see a boy pulling a wheelbarrow, I look into the shop windows and see myself in the mirror. So that's you, you're free, you're walking. I see tarmac under my feet, grey and wet, a dog sniffs at a streetlamp, I see cars coming towards me, I hear the clatter of the local train high above me, yellow carriages move brightly by. People hurry past me. I'm so greedy for the world; I'm tasting the world again, this grey, gloomy, ugly Berlin, these walls and railway arches, these bridges and pubs. I read the adverts: Schultheiss-Patzenhofer, I read: Singer, I read: Brauhaus Tempelhof. Everything is there again, and it is like a present. Freedom – that's the world in which we can lose and find ourselves.

Now you must relearn the old words and gestures. You're free. You need to learn once more to reach into your trouser pocket, take out your wallet, open it and look for coins. You knew it all once, now you have to learn it again. At Friedrichstrasse station you must step up to the counter and say loudly: One ticket to Eichkamp, third class! You must say it quite calmly. No one should notice that this is new for you, and that you're doing it for the first time. You've done it before. Everything should be as it always was.

As always I go to Aschinger, I stand at the counter, people crowding around me, and I join the queue. A fat woman at the front is dishing out soup. I'm hungry, hungry for the world and pea soup, and then I hear myself saying: 'Erbsenbrei with bacon,' and then I move away with my plate and stand at one of these tables, blow to cool the soup and think: Nothing is better than Erbsenbrei. Erbsenbrei is my favourite dish.

I stand at the ticket counter in Friedrichstrasse station. I clearly hear myself saying: 'One for Eichkamp, third class.' It sounds so strange to me. A woman throws me a yellow ticket – women are working everywhere now – coins roll over the brass plate, spin, tip, roll, fall on the floor. I bend down, hastily pick them up and feel my fingers shaking; I wrap my hand around the yellow bit of cardboard and run off and then stand on the escalator that carries me slowly upstairs. Upstairs everything is as it always was. They have put up the green sign: Spandau West. My God, I was sitting in Moabit, but here, all the time, trains have been going to Potsdam, to Lichtenrade, to Gleisdreieck, to Erkner, and every ten minutes there's one to Spandau West. How can that be? Where does the time go? Where has it gone?

So I will go to Eichkamp. I will sit in the local train compartment as always, the houses and walls and streets of the city fly past the window – an ancient melody: Zoo, Savignyplatz, Charlottenburg, Westkreuz, Eichkamp. I will get off there, I will walk through the estate and then stand in front of our house – of course. I will ring the bell and wait, and my heart will be thumping, and I will say: I'm here, and

I will be a bit embarrassed. My mother will wrap me in her arms, she will do it with her beautiful and yet rather theatrical gestures and she will sigh: My child, my son, my dear child! And I will stand there, quite stiff and rigid, and think: I'm here. Am I here?

Last memory of his Reich: an act of protest. We've dug holes with shovels, with picks and axes, and we crouch in them like trees meant to be planted in an avenue the next day. We're at the Dortmund–Ems Canal. We're supposed to hold the Ruhr District. We crouch in deep, damp, sticky holes. Light drizzle falls. We are called Task Force Grasmehl and are all that remains of a paratroop regiment: about a hundred men who have been quickly rounded up in Brandenburg over the last few days. In fact, we're from a convalescent unit. We're all sick, wounded, exhausted, convalescents in between wards. We hardly have any weapons, but we do have bandages around our bellies and our thighs, plasters on our backs, diet notes in our pockets: Task Force Grasmehl vs the United States of America.

In Brandenburg they had told us: 'You're being transferred now, you're on your way to a convalescent home.' On the railway ramp there were lots of boxcars, an endless train of rusty brown wagons. We were loaded on our train, with luggage and marching rations and a few guns, but then nothing happened. No locomotive. That puzzled me. The whole morning I crept around suspiciously at the ramp, looking out for a locomotive. I said to myself: This is important now. This will decide the rest of your life. The ring around his Reich is nice and tight now, Greater Germany still extends from the Oder to the Rhine. And if the locomotive that they attach now comes from the direction of Berlin, we're off to fight the Russians. You'll be labouring for many years in Russia. But if the locomotive comes from the direction of Magdeburg you'll be off to fight the Yanks, and with that I associated very little, hardly anything.

In the late afternoon, I had dozed off in my corner of the wagon, the train suddenly lurched forwards: a hard blow, a roar of iron, a squeak, a crunch as if a rusty chain were suddenly being pulled tight. We're moving, I wake up with a start, look out, we're heading westwards. Fine, westwards it is. We were loaded off the train in Unna. When we marched through the town we passed by some barracks. The SS were quartered there, and when they heard our weary and poor marching steps, they leapt, plunged, flew to the windows with frightened, searching expressions. SS men with big, frightened eyes, their jackets unbuttoned; some had just washed, they had hurried to the window in their underwear, one of them held a razor up to us as if pleading, foam around his mouth, shaving foam. But no, not yet: we may look similar, but we're not Americans. You still have time. You can still retreat. That was my first surprise after so many years: SS frightened, SS in flight.

Our task was to cover the retreat of the SS units at the Dortmund–Ems Canal. That was why we were sitting here in these muddy holes, that was why we were getting large quantities of biscuits and beer and cigarettes. But we had no weapons. The others over there had those. Over there, on the other bank, there was nothing to see, nothing but grey furrowed fields, fields in March, but somewhere in the hinterland they must have had enormous amounts of cannon and heavy weaponry lined up and ready. With those they were digging up and combing our position, metre by metre. Three or four times a day the firing broke over us: a hurricane of fire and steel, stones and spraying soil. Were we supposed to throw back beer bottles? Sometimes someone cried out, sometimes body parts flew through the air, and then peace prevailed again. Someone whimpered nearby, and a motorbike drove up, they pulled the wounded man out and a new one was put in the hole. That's how it was. That's how four days and nights passed.

On the fifth day I was detailed. A motorbike messenger came and shouted something in my ear. I had been put on food-fetching duty. Had I understood correctly? I let a few moments pass, then got to my feet feeling stiff as a tree, crept back, crawled through wet grass, past rubble and churned-up streets. I got back to my feet behind a ruined building and took my bearings. It must have been a school once, because shiny desks stood at angles in the field. The feeling of being back at school. I sat down at one of the desks, took a deep breath and looked up at the sky, which hung over us grey and damp as a linen sheet, and thought: Easter – of course, it's Easter Sunday today. My God, once upon a time that really did exist: a proper Easter. That was when you put on your Sunday best early in the morning, went to church, you looked for eggs in the garden, red, blue and green ones, then you had coffee in the dining room, and Wieman recited Goethe on the radio: 'Released from the ice are stream and brook.' After that Elly Ney played something powerful by Beethoven.*

Now that's all over. No more Goethe and Beethoven, no resurrection. Now all the cannon in the world are turned on Germany. The end is there, the real end of the world, as it says in the Bible: flames will fall from heaven and you will freeze as Lot's wife froze. The Reich is breaking apart, Hitler's Reich, our Reich, the German Reich is breaking apart. Now there will be nothing but dying. Thank God: the German Reich is finally breaking apart. The food depot was like all the food depots in the world. They will survive all the Armageddons. A basement, gloomy passageways, storerooms, counters, warning signs, a regimental order still flapping from a black-board. A fat lance corporal squats weary and plump like a grocer behind his tins, with a pencil tucked in his ear like a shop boy; after a lot of toing and froing, with condescending indifference he shoves bread and bits of sausage and a mas-sive lump of margarine towards me. Cigarettes on top, jam on top of that, bottles of beer. I let it all land in my tarpaulin, throw it over my back like a sack and trot back.

Fog and damp are rising from the ground now. It's barely five o'clock and already it's nearly dark. A machine gun putters away somewhere in the distance. I sink into the slip-pery, muddy soil. Our bunker is right beside the ruins of the school. Something like a unit command post has been improvised here for Task Force Grasmehl. In a ruined house whose bare walls reach into the sky, there is some kind of office. Two sergeants sit around here, twitchily cranking away at a field telephone: 'Can you hear us? Task Force Grasmehl here! Hello, is that the division?' I deliver my stuff and try to give something like a salute. I've never managed to do that in a proper soldierly way, but the two men on the phone don't seem to care much any more. They say: 'Right then, now clear off!' They say it as if talking to a dog, and ignore my miserable civilian manners. It's a clear sign: when German sergeants turn human, a world war is lost.

Suddenly, outside behind the house, I get a big shock. Even today I haven't forgotten it, I will never forget it. Hermann Suhren is standing by a wall and looks almost like Jesus. They've taken off his belt buckle and ripped off his lance corporal's stripes and wrapped a white cloth around his eyes. He looks like a wounded man who has just had a bandage put on his head, and he had in fact been wounded: a year ago at Monte Cassino, with me, that was Easter too, Easter 1944, we were both wounded during the charge on Peak 503 just below the monastery. We had seen each other again in the field hospital in Bolzano and then, in Germany, we had become friends. We had come here together from Brandenburg a week before. Hermann was a clockmaker from somewhere in Westphalia, he was Catholic in that dull and loyal way that lads from Westphalia often are, which made him immune to the stubborn fanaticism of those who still believed in final victory. 'Lad,' he often said to me, 'if that goes wrong – O God, O God!'

Now they're shooting him. A paratroop lieutenant stands twenty metres in front of him, with two corporals beside him. The lieutenant holds his sub-machine gun stretched across shoulder and hip. I don't know him, I've never seen him before, he looks slim and blond and wiry, like all the lieutenants in the world, and as I'm about to throw myself in between them – Hermann, what is it, what are they doing to you, this is impossible, it must be a mistake – I suddenly hear the sub-machine gun barking loudly, a crazy burst of fire, only five or six shots, very short, very concise and precisely aimed, and I see Hermann Suhren slumping silently against the wall. He falls slowly forward like a sack of flour, bends double, plunges head first into the mud, lands with a splash, doesn't make a sound. I know bullets are a painless way to die. You just feel a dull blow, nothing more.

Later I learned something of what had happened. He had crept out of his hole and hadn't been found at his post for half a day, and had disappeared behind this ruined house. Even now I don't know whether he was just seeking shelter, sensible, soldierly shelter from the hurricane of iron that was raining down on us, or whether he didn't want to go on fighting. His home village wasn't far away. By that time everything was on the point of collapse, the war was nearing chaos, a confusion of individuals, whether escaping, retreating or holding out to the bitter end. Some went on stubbornly fighting, some still believed in victory, and in between everyone was trying to save his own skin. But somebody had caught him. One of those blond, Nordic gods, to whom the war had given birth and carried aloft, had caught him sleeping in the ruined house, about three hundred metres behind the front line, had turned him into a case of absence without leave, a case of cowardice in the face of the enemy, a case of desertion, and was now making short work of him. That was permitted. There were such orders in those days, mad orders from the dark man in Berlin, to keep the discipline and morale of the troops intact. The matter was almost legal at the time; any officer could shoot any fleeing soldier at the time.

But for me it was the moment when I woke up, when I jolted awake out of my four-year soldierly sleep, when I said: It's over, it's finished, you're not staying another day among these people. It was my second of truth. Suddenly there was only rage and hatred and protest in me: Hermann, they've killed you now, you from Monte Cassino, you from Westphalia, they have shot millions of people, we have all fired shots, our hands are all covered with blood. Europe is a bloodbath, Fortress Europe is a slaughterhouse;* and slowly everyone here is going to be killed by everyone else. War has become a revolting senseless carnage, as revolting as our German mythology: bloody Walstatt, King Etzel's death and Kriemhild and Siegfried and grief over Valhalla. Oh, that people that I belong to. What is it about this people that it lets itself be slaughtered so bloodily, that it shoots and stabs, slays and murders its own citizens at the last minute? I hate that people with its Nibelungen loyalty, with its air of heroic greatness, with its dark Richard Wagner face, that gang of murderers, those journeyman butchers who, here on this stage of history, disguised as generals and military judges, are playing out an ancient German Nibelungen saga, the *Götterdämmerung* somewhere near Lünen.* I don't want to be a German any more. I want to leave this people. I'm crossing to the other side.

None of this sounds very glorious, I know. It's five to twelve. The Reich is falling to bits like an old cupboard. They've divided it up at Yalta long ago. In Berlin the powerful men have carried with them for weeks the little glass capsules that they will bite on when they have reached their destination after their infernal gallop through history. In four weeks they will bite. At this moment, as the universal nightmare begins to fade, when even the blind can see again, you cross over, you, a little Wehrmacht corporal, twenty-five years old, one of twenty million men in uniform, and you step all alone in front of the United States of America and say: I don't want to do this any more, I can't do this any more. I am coming out of hatred for Hitler and out of rage and despair over my people. That damned German loyalty! I know that this pose comes a little too late, it almost has a whiff of ingratiation about it. It's not working any more. You should go down with them. They will only grin and say: Take a look at these Germans, now they come creeping up one by one, claiming they had always been against it. A revolting, subject people. Now that anti-fascism is for sale on the markets of the world at knock-down prices, they are betraying their own cause. A revolting case of betrayal.

Still, I did go over to the other side back then. I was full of hatred, I had awoken from the lethargy of my soldier's life, I was wide awake and said to myself: Something has to happen now. You have to do something now. You can't join in any more. I crept back into my hole. Darkness had already fallen on the Dortmund–Ems Canal, I slipped right into the muddy hollow, I let myself fall, I picked up my rifle and held it ready to shoot, I was willing to shoot; but it was a pointless action, we sat there like cardboard dummies and for two days we had had no rifle ammunition. Sometimes when they fired tracer bullets from the other side it was suddenly as bright as day, and for a few seconds everything looked like a battlefield in a performance of Shakespeare: *Macbeth* in Giessen or Bad Kissingen. Why do Armageddons always have this hint of provincial theatre productions about them? Is world history essentially a Puccini opera?

A newcomer now squatted in the hole next to me. A young lad, early twenties, intelligent farming face, black shock of hair that I suddenly see when in the midst of the gunfire he takes his helmet off. Is he insane? In amongst the exploding shells he has set up a tiny pocket mirror in front of him, he takes a comb from his trouser pocket, wets it with spittle and begins to do his hair, he is only interested in his straight parting, he fiddles around with his appearance like a young playboy in the bathroom before hitting town in the evening. A real Narcissus in the final German battle. Good God, put your helmet back on! There's shrapnel flying around like midges at the Wannsee in autumn, leave your face, the enemy will be down here any minute in any case. Stop playing the matinee idol of the trenches: Eros and Thanatos, a young German ready to die casually grooms himself, a subject from Böcklin or Feuerbach.* That's another of those terrible Puccini-esque ideas taken from German bourgeois Romanticism: beauty and death as twin brothers. Once again there's that provincial flavour to Germany's downfall. The Lord up there, the one who's supposed to be running the whole show according to Hegel, must be a very strange man, directing a shoddy farce from his divine throne. World history: nothing but a disgusting bit of am-dram.

But then I suddenly realise: he's the right one, yes, him. The Reich can't matter all that much to him. And while the evening rations are being doled out, and while we fumble in the dark for sausage and beer and jam, I lean over to him and say casually, with my mouth full: 'I'm clearing off tonight. You coming with me?' I've never been a good soldier, but I know that you can't undertake these border-crossings on your own. There have to be two of you. Then you can help each other. On your own you're always lost. And the fellow looks at me with a grin and in disbelief, he's put his helmet back on some time ago, and asks in amazement: 'Christ, just cross over? To the Yanks? Are you crazy?' 'Yes,' I say, 'tonight. You can come along if you want.' He mumbled something to himself that could mean one thing or another. Right now he seemed to be more interested in his bit of sausage. There are unbending rules in war, tactical rules that you can always depend on, and one of them is that even the worst artillery barrage stops soon after midnight. Then you have peace until dawn. It's when the heroes want to get some sleep. When the illuminated numbers on my watch showed three o'clock exactly, I climbed out of my hole, silently got my kit together, gave him a kick and whispered: 'Right, come on!' And he gets up as if in a dream, perhaps he's been sleeping, and comes creeping after me. Strange, I think, you just have to give them a kick and say: 'Come on,' and they follow you to the ends of the earth.

We advance like predators in the jungle, metre after metre to the bank of the canal. Ahead of us is a bridge, a narrow iron viaduct that was blown up long ago; the black struts have fallen into the canal. From our side you can get across hand over hand. In the darkness all we can see is a shattered pillar and that skewed steel railing that must end somewhere in the water. We'll see. It feels like being in the jungle. We now hang like monkeys from that slippery black strut, clawing on to the sides and climbing down hand over hand. Farewell, my dearest fatherland – didn't I once learn that song in school?

Suddenly there's an almighty splash, I feel water, let myself go, stand up to my belt buckle in water, but no deeper, a rushing gurgle around me. My God, we're giving ourselves away. Everyone around here must have heard that. They had. All of a sudden there was gunfire, a machine gun from our side, a few rifles barked briefly. Then it went quiet again. It was probably a routine response from the sentries. We stood in the water like that for a small eternity and didn't dare to move, trembling with cold and fear. God, what if they catch us now? You haven't even got any ammunition left to fire back. But no, they're not going to get you. You'd rather go under, drown or pull the rifle from their hands, hit them in the face with the stock and shoot yourself. You're not going to take me alive, gentlemen. It's over. I've made up my mind. I would rather be dead than be a German soldier for a moment longer. The bridge has collapsed, I'm already standing deep in the water, I'm swimming to the west, so farewell – I'm going to the enemy.

Easter night on the Dortmund–Ems Canal. The water is rising and sometimes bubbles out with a gurgle from my high boots. The Lord is risen, he is risen indeed. They have shot Hermann, everybody's being shot now, I want no more of this, I can do no more, I was once a soldier, I was once a student from Berlin, whose parents placed high hopes on him. Now the dark man is in Berlin and letting everything burn. In the end he will burn himself. We have been caught up in the mills of history, we middle-class children from Hamburg and Breslau, we German sons, every one of us is being ground up individually, like a thousand grains of wheat, we are being crushed to pieces and stirred into the cake of history. Now the others are stirring the cake: the Americans and the Russians, the British and the French, and the Germans are being crushed. Thank heavens: the Germans have had it in history. I have left my people. I'm free.

And then all of a sudden – probably more than an hour had passed – we were actually standing on the opposite shore. We were standing in the land of the enemy. I was twenty-five, dripping with water, shivering with cold and fear, and standing for the first time on German soil free of Hitler. German soil free of Hitler? Take a look at it, the dark, winter-washed grassy ground beneath our feet, take a look at it, these few square metres of Westphalian soil; enemy territory, it exists, it no longer belongs to him, on the ground on which you are now standing there are no longer any SS, there are no longer any military judges. German soil free of Hitler, a free Germany in the dark of night, can there even be such a thing? Your whole youth has been put into reverse: that Germany can be torn from him, it is possible. Throw yourself down, kiss the ground and say: He is risen. Come on, Jürgen, join in: He is risen indeed.

We didn't throw ourselves down, we didn't kiss the ground, but I know that I said to Jürgen: 'Come on, throw that away!' And we took our rifles and our steel helmets, our sidearms and gas masks, and dropped them on the ground which was free of Hitler. I was fourteen years old when Hitler came to power; I had known only this Reich, his Reich, our Reich, I had only known hatred and war and us all having to sacrifice ourselves down to the very last one. I had only ever heard that outside the Jews, the Bolsheviks, the plutocrats were in charge, all enemies, all savages, all Untermenschen who wanted to crush and destroy our poor, proud country. I had never seen an American or a Russian. I actually had no idea who I was crossing over to and what awaited me when I got there. All I knew was: here, for the first time, is Germany without Hitler, here is soil that he no longer rules. His power is broken. This soil is good.

So no Easter greeting, no Easter grace, but something like a childlike dance of joy: Boy, Jürgen, we did it! We're free, we're not soldiers any more, the war is over! Do you know what that means: the war is over? The war is like a poisonous black cloud that comes over peoples, it paralyses, it dazzles, you can't resist it. But now we have resisted it, we have broken out of that circle of death, we have outwitted the fate of peoples. We couldn't prevent this war, of course we couldn't, but we could bring it to an end. All by ourselves. That is our achievement, our deed. Tonight, Easter night 1945, the war between Germany and the world was ended, and the two of us did it.

We're like two generals on our way to sign the capitulation document. Our real generals aren't doing it, they're still fighting for Hitler, so we have to do it, Jürgen, you and me. Two corporals go to the enemy and say: The Second World War is over. We capitulate in the name of Germany. Because our leaders aren't doing it.

We had already been on the move for half an hour; we were walking cross-country, walking like proper civilians, we thought something was bound to happen now, but nothing did. Behind us to the east the sky was already beginning to brighten. The Americans plainly weren't planning to sacrifice their soldiers in close combat. Their heavy artillery was a long way back, and there were perhaps a few sentries and mortars in between – no more than that.

It was a damp and foggy April morning at around five, no longer night, but not yet day either, the time of day at which you normally feel terribly hungover if you're on guard duty, neither asleep nor awake but both at the same time. My God, how often did you stand guard at five o'clock in the morning in Russia and, with a nauseating taste in your mouth, watch the sunrise, the awakening day and think: How long is this business with Hitler going to go on for? Nowhere in the world are there more beautiful, broad, fantastical sunrises than over Russia's plains. It's a blaze of colour from reddish purple to bright yellow, a real struggle between light and darkness as if in the desert. Yes, perhaps in the desert the sun is as big as it is over Russia. That's a long time ago. The Germans were driven out of Russia ages ago, they were driven out of the desert, now the Germans stand on guard here, and here in Germany everything is small and cramped, dark and damp: here the sun goes up and down without grandeur.

Suddenly I hear something rattling and pattering. 'Stop, Jürgen,' I say, 'don't move. Can't you hear it? I don't think that's something in the bushes.' And suddenly a group appears out of the morning mist. I have never seen an American soldier before, I have no idea what they look like, and yet I know straight away: here they are – of course. They emerge like ghosts from the darkness, stand huge before us like poplars in the night, two black and two white men in grey-green field uniform, sub-machine guns in their arms, grenades on their belts, helmets casually shoved back, they're trotting to the front like that, and when they suddenly spot us they get a massive shock. 'Oh, Germans!' one of them exclaims and whistles through his teeth, and the men behind him are already raising their hands, they're ready to surrender on the spot, thinking they've run into the hands of a German shock troop. They'd rather be taken prisoner – safety first. We're both wet and bare-headed, we have no weapons and we do our best to make it clear to them that we want them to take us prisoner, not the other way around. It's so hard to explain the swapped roles. It takes a while. My school English proves extremely poor when I try to make them understand. I know Shakespeare and a bit of Milton, I've studied English for nine years, but I hadn't learned how to express all the things I wanted to about Hermann Suhren, about our generals and Hitler, and how it was time for peace. I paraphrased, garbled and stammered something together. They gradually understood and nodded, one of them laughed briefly and thoughtfully scratched the back of his neck, and after a while the leader said: 'OK.' I didn't understand that phrase, I had never heard it, but then the others put us between them, said: 'Come on, let's go,' and moved off with us. Farewell, then, now we're firmly in the enemy's hands. We've done it.

For all foreigners America is a genuine wonder. When the ship docks in Manhattan in the morning, what awaits the traveller is a broad, bold, reasonable and fantastical world. I had never seen it, and still – my sense of wonder was greater, my America more astonishing. I switched directly from Unna and Lünen to the States, I had come from Hitler's Reich, it was like a sudden cut in the film of time.

We're standing in a US Army command post in an old farmhouse, but inside it's like a strange mixture of tennis club and aeroplane cockpit, a lot of soldiers, both white and black, a lot of telephones and walkie-talkies, some wear headphones, and at the same time all are listening to a portable radio that's playing jazz. They're all well dressed and healthy, their movements loose and springy. They behave like a sports team and they're all wearing very tight trousers and grey-green shirts. I keep looking for epaulettes – I can't tell who's an officer and who's a private. I just stand there in astonishment, watching the way they talk to each other: briefly and laconically; how they smoke: deliberately and with a hint of addiction; how they speak on the telephone: resolute and yet very relaxed. Some of them have a smart smile playing around their lips when they talk; they're always smiling. Others are quite merry, like little boys playing cowboys and Indians. Is it a merry war over here? I don't know, it's all so confusing and strange to me. I just know all of a sudden, even before I've uttered a word, what kind of a stale, dreadful, rancid world I've come from. Back there, all the soldiers have a side parting, they have spots on their faces, their expressions are pinched, they stand to attention and make others stand to attention before their glittering epaulettes: they shout. People have always shouted in Germany: the Führer shouted at the Gauleiter, the generals at the officers, the officers at the sergeants, and my NCO shouted at me: You ass! And you're supposed to be a student?

And now here I stand, Germany's most pitiful son, a turncoat and a traitor. I'm standing in a dirty, wet uniform, dripping water on the floor; my face is damp and muddy, my hands black with soil. I don't even have a cap any more, I look like a rain-drenched dog that's been dragged from the gutter, and I hear myself saying very quietly: 'I have come of my own free will. I have brought Jürgen Lubahn from Lübeck with me. We hate this war. We hate Hitler. We're only convalescents. If you stop firing your terrible weapons, gentlemen, I will explain our positions to you, the little that I know. But you've now got to stop this carnage. We have no ammunition left.'

I really did say 'gentlemen' – 'meine Herren' – and I said it all in German because after a few attempts in English the uniformed man who was interrogating me – he seemed to be a lieutenant – said: 'You may speak German. This is

Mr Levison. He studied in Heidelberg with Mr Weber and Mr Jaspers. He will interpret.'

I know it sounds a little absurd and strange, but that's how it was, that's exactly how it was. I had come over from the filth of the trench war to the enemy side, I was a philosophy student, and the first words, the first names that this enemy said to me were Mr Weber and Mr Jaspers.* Nobody in my unit had ever heard the names of philosophers and sociologists. As far as paratroopers were concerned, the mind didn't exist. It was a world of mercenaries and adventurers, they said 'shit', pulled a face, then yelled and drank beer.

And then there was a long conversation between Mr Levison and me. As long as I live I will never forget it, a little colloquium on Easter Monday 1945, at seven in the morning. He said Heidelberg and I said Freiburg. He said Jaspers, and I said Heidegger. 'Before I was conscripted,' I said, 'I studied with Heidegger for a term: about the principle of reason.' He found that hugely interesting. He was obviously a German Jew, one of those who had managed to emigrate. He wasn't a soldier, he was accompanying the troops as a civilian on interpreting duties and as a specialist on Germany. He loved Germany, and was very happy to have found among all the uniformed men someone who had studied the same subject. And now he and I began a lengthy discussion about Heidegger and Jaspers, where they agreed and what their differences were. We talked about Dasein analysis and the mysticism of Being, and about ontological difference, and in between there were reports from the front, the radio was still playing jazz, and then we talked about whether Being could be explained by Dasein. Heidegger hadn't yet made his great 'turn'.*

Yes, that was how it was on that Easter Monday in '45. Everything seemed a bit fantastical to me, a bit dreamlike: I had abandoned my people and my fatherland, and now I found it here in an enemy command post. They know our minds, they know something about our philosophies and our thinkers, and Mr Levison's eyes turned quite misty at the word 'Heidelberg', and he started warning me about Heidegger. That was a dark German path, and not to be compared with the expanse and brightness of Alfred Weber. But Jürgen Lubahn was still standing next to me with his dark, wet shock of hair. Did he still have his mirror on him? It must all have seemed incomprehensible to him, like a secret conspiracy. There were the black soldiers and the other army boys, drinking instant coffee, smoking cigarettes, and now the officer wanted to know about our positions. It was already light outside, but we talked only about German philosophy and why Germany had come to such a terrible end. And I thought all of a sudden: You see, it really exists, you've always looked for something like that and you didn't know if it even existed. My God, how can that be? You've lived for twenty-five years in Germany, four of them in the Wehrmacht, you've always been silent, you always put up with everything, you never felt at home in Germany, and you've only been with the enemy for an hour and already you feel at home. You're no longer alone in the world. The enemy – that's your world.

Then everything happened thick and fast. The ice was broken, and now a whole flood wanted to spill forth. I told the Americans about our positions. I said: 'They're over there, and there, and they have a mortar there and an anti-tank gun there, of our hundred or so men many still have rifles, but only a few have even two or three rounds of ammunition. And there are no heavy weapons left at all. In the hinterland everyone's beginning to flee. Don't fire your heavy weapons.' And barely twenty minutes later silence did indeed fall on our section of the front. Suddenly it was quiet, and I thought: You did that, this is your Easter peace.

They had silenced their artillery and quickly put together a special unit; they went across as a shock troop, and it wasn't ten o'clock or half past yet, they came back, a huge troop now as if after an unexpectedly successful fishing trip. They brought our whole squad with them, they had simply taken them prisoner. How am I ever supposed to forget that moment? Uwe and Heinz, Fritz and Peter, you lads from Brandenburg and Berlin, from Munich and Hamburg – now you're all coming in as prisoners. And you stand there, leaning against a military vehicle, smoking a cigarette they gave you: Lucky Strike, your thirty pieces of silver, of course you've betrayed them but you also didn't betray them. You've got them out of that bloody Fortress Europe, you saved them from the blood soup that the dark man in Berlin is now boiling up from all of us. The Germans aren't worthy of his tragedy any more. They walk past me, beaten and mute, a people seduced, they walk like all the prisoners in the world: weary, exhausted and dull. They don't realise that you are the reason they are here. They think you arrived a few minutes earlier. Who knows during such an Armageddon who is first and who is last? They didn't notice your escape. They will never know that one of their corporals ended the Second World War here on the Dortmund–Ems Canal, on a stretch only a kilometre wide. Not very much, a kilometre; but still. It will stay my secret.

In the afternoon we were assembled into companies of prisoners. A sergeant came and said: 'Take that guy out!' So I was brought back to Mr Levison and the lieutenant. The troop was now in motion, they were setting off to advance across the Ruhr District and further into Germany. From the Ruhr to Hitler was only four weeks. And the lieutenant said: 'We thank you. That was good. But now we can't help you any more. You're going into captivity now, a prisoner like all the others. Is that clear?' And after a moment's hesitation he said: 'Give me your pay book, I'd like at least to write something in it. Maybe it will help you in your dealings with us one day.' And he took my pay book, opened it at the first page and wrote beneath my number in pencil and in small Latin letters four words which made me feel a little embarrassed and upset. My God, that's such nonsense, I thought. Still, I thought later, no German officer would ever have written that about you. And I wasn't yet out of the command post when a black soldier came and said: 'Give me your watch, give me your money, come on, get a move on, damn it.' In soldiers' slang this is called filching, and I gave him the watch, gave him the money, and knew all of a sudden that I was now a prisoner of war like millions of other Germans.

The wonderful, incomprehensible freedom of captivity began. A time of suffering commenced, which was full of hope. I was now living among crowds, among weary, dull, hungry bunches of people who were shoved from camp to camp, from cage to cage; and yet, in the middle of this big grey army of prisoners, I came to life for the first time. I felt that my time had come: You're going to wake up, you're going to come into your own. Had Hitler been victorious that would never have happened. We're right at the bottom now, but there is hope in being at the bottom, there is future, there are opportunities. You're in a bad way, but you know that it can get better now. It will get better. For the first time I experienced what the future really means: the hope that things will be better tomorrow than they are today. The future – that would never have existed under Hitler.

We had been brought to France, to the camp at Cherbourg. Countless millions now fell into the hands of the Allies, and they didn't know how to deal with the sudden, crazed

133

self-liquidation of a huge, humiliated people. There was a lot of hunger, misery and rain. We stood in a field, we stood crammed closely together, I didn't even have a coat now, we stood there for days and nights, and there's hardly anything more terrible than standing for a night in a wet field and then another night; we walked up and down, we wrapped ourselves in jackets and blankets. People now threw away their medals and epaulettes. The ground was awash with NCOs' braids and Iron Crosses, we walked on them, and in among them were old fifty-mark notes. It was all worthless now, we heard, and if we got hold of a cigarette we enjoyed lighting it with a rolled-up ten-mark note, rolled into a spill; it seemed a cheap and arrogant source of pleasure.

Things started happening now. One day in Cherbourg, we get a newspaper for prisoners, and in that newspaper it says in big letters: 'Hitler dead'. He had died in the battle for Berlin, it said. Dönitz had taken control of the Reich government.* And indeed, there was a list of the new cabinet led by Admiral Dönitz. Some people now awoke from their lethargy, many didn't believe the newspaper, and most were left entirely indifferent, but for me it was another moment of astonishment. I still see myself lying in the big tent that we have now been given. It's a beautiful, sunny morning in May, it's already quite warm; the others are outside, sitting on rocks, lurking for food, rolling something smokable out of any bits of straw they can find, brooding, and I hold this paper in my hands and can't understand that such a thing exists: paper printed in German, a whole newspaper that wasn't made by the Nazis. A real German newspaper without hatred or oaths of loyalty or an insistence on the final German victory. It's like a miracle: that a German language is possible without Hitler, that it can exist against him, that it can be done: German letters, German sentences against Hitler.

When I started reading my first newspaper, he was already in power, and I knew only a standardised, belligerent, triumphalist press: the *Völkischer Beobachter* and the *Lokal-Anzeiger*, *Angriff* and the *Deutsche Allgemeine Zeitung*. It always seemed quite clear to me that he had also defeated the German language and now kept it under occupation, and my parents had always said to me: 'What the papers say isn't true, but you mustn't say so. Outside you must always pretend that you believe everything.' To me the German language had become identical with lies. You can only speak truthfully in private. What the papers say is always a lie, but you mustn't say so. And now here I was holding a newspaper in my hands, which was in German and didn't lie. How was that possible? How can language and truth coincide? How can it be that you can believe what is printed? It was the first free German newspaper in my life.

It was only later that I understood what it had actually said. It was the following night. We were lying in a big tent, lying packed side by side on the bare ground of France. No one could turn around without moving their neighbour too; it was a complicated kind of collective sleep. I had awoken from troubled dreams and suddenly, in the dark, saw that headline again in front of me in huge letters and thought: You did it! You actually experienced it! He's really dead, and no paratrooper and no bearer of the Knight's Cross will ever be able to bring him back to life. Hitler is dead – do you hear that? His power is over, he has passed like all creation, he too had to die, even Hitler is mortal. How come that even the powerful must die? Haven't they defeated death? Be honest: you never thought it possible. You never hoped he would die, you always believed that he was the more powerful, bigger, stronger than you. He or you – it was always decided in his favour. You knew as early as 1941 that he wouldn't win, it was clear when he declared war on Russia and America that he couldn't win. But you always had a dark certainty that he would do it, that he would be able to stretch his defeat out for a long, perhaps an infinitely long time. Europe at the time was a fortress, the Allies were advancing slowly and without any victories. He had us all in his iron grip. We were all his workers, his soldiers, his slaves and servants.

I'm standing guard in Paris by the gate of the Lariboisière Hospital, from which one can, surprisingly, see the white dome of Sacré-Coeur. It's Christmas 1941, it's cold and windy, snow sweeps down the boulevard, and I think: That's how it's always going to be from now on, in winter and in summer. He's defeated you, he's defeated us all, the whole of Europe lies at his feet. We lie in bunkers and graves for him, we dig and shoot for Hitler; the whole of Europe is one single gun emplacement which he will hold for decades. You will turn thirty and forty, he's already robbed you of your youth, he will rob you of your whole life; he will fall one day, but you will fall first. You don't have the strength any more. The Continent is a bivouac in the German thirty years' war. That did happen; that had happened before. You can stand it for perhaps two or three years – not more. You will take your own life, you'd rather shoot yourself; you were just born at the wrong time.

That's it. You were born under Adolf Hitler. You'll die under him too. It's not your world, not your century. Give yourself up, let yourself fall. Perhaps other parents will give birth to you in other times. This isn't your time. It's Hitler's time. And now he was suddenly dead, the fortress was broken, the castle was taken, the ring was broken, the demon had been overpowered. Hitler was dead and I was alive. I felt as if I had just been born that night. Now life was bound to begin.

Further miracles followed every day. One morning an officer came, accompanied by two soldiers; they had big lists with them, and now they started taking soundings. They started looking for Nazis and the victims of Nazis, SS men and resistance fighters were to be identified. We had to strip to the waist, and under that examination I learned for the first time that there were Germans who as members of the SS wore a tattoo with their blood group, and others who had numbers branded into their lower arms. Now the two were separated, and there was a barbed-wire camp to which the ones with the blood-group tattoo were sent and another one to which those with the numbers on their arms were led. The camp with the SS men was still half-empty, even then everyone claimed not to have been part of it all. It was right next to our camp, and in the evening I could see them squatting on rocks in there. They were thin, resigned fellows who sat around, dogged and defiant, staring straight ahead, perhaps still hoping for some miraculous turnaround. They had lost their game. They had survived. That hadn't been part of their plan: to survive Hitler. Now they had to pay for it. Sometimes one of our guards came and spat at them; and the others, those with the numbers, were given little favours, they got more to smoke and had duties assigned to them.

What filled me wasn't a feeling of revenge or triumph. We were all prisoners, German prisoners, a beaten people, we all ate the same gruel of defeat. But the fact that this defeat also brought justice was another incomprehensible experience for me. I stand by the gate of our cage, fences and barbed wire are around me, there are other cages next to our cage, other camps beyond our camp. As far as I can see, only rocks, wire and wooden sheds behind which there are yet more cages. Watchtowers at its corners, the world is a camp behind whose barbed wire people are crouching.

Along the big camp road scattered with gravel stones new transports are now arriving daily, drifting past me like huge weary herds. They have now sorted out the ranks; since yesterday it's only been officers who come, endless processions, thousands of them push their way slowly past me like a sluggish grey mass. They still wear their epaulettes, they still look well fed, they come five abreast with dull, defeated expressions, they wear field-grey and green and blue coats, and some have fat bellies. And walking beside them are their black guards, violently driving them on like watchdogs with their 'Come on! Let's go!', sometimes, when the endless procession almost comes to a standstill, beating them on the back with little rods with a whack: Germany, here come your gentlemen, your glory is over, a thousand officers are being led to water like a weary herd, a beaten leadership, yesterday's elite. Sometimes there are faces that look like Prittwitz, von Kleist and von Retzow, they're carrying Pomerania's and Brandenburg's pride to the grave, the sons of Prussian noblemen who swore fealty to the dark man in Berlin and are now being led by black men into big cages like wild animals. They had already lost their honour, the majors of the Luftwaffe and the captains of the army. Now come men with gold epaulettes, they must be generals, and among them others with red-braided trousers, they are general staff officers. Our paratroop lieutenant will also be there somewhere, the one who shot Hermann Suhren; he had already lost his honour. And now all of them, five men in a row, are drifting, dusty and torn and numb, into big cages. This is how a wild people is led into captivity.

And I stand there by my gate and think: This picture isn't new. For thousands of years peoples have been beaten like that, armies defeated, and the victor always assumes the right to declare his victory to be that of the good cause, his triumph a triumph of justice. That's the sublime lie of world history, the right of might. It has never been true, we know that. But look: this time it really is true. This one time it is really true that our guards have represented the good and the men out there the bad. Now, in our broken Fortress Europe the jails and prisons, the camps and death factories are being opened, the victims saved, the dead honoured, the persecutors punished. Never before has there been such a thing on earth. Look at it, cling tightly to it, never forget it in your life: there was once a war that the Germans and Hitler lost, and in their defeat the order of the world was restored. Good was powerful, evil was defeated. There was justice in the world. It's almost like the Day of Judgement: the mills of death stand still, now the sheep are being separated from the goats, the persecutors from the persecuted, a big book is opened up.

And I thought: So you've survived Hitler. One day you will be released from Cherbourg. You will start living, you will learn, work, have a job, you will get older and slowly forget your youth under Hitler. But not this, not this one hour in Cherbourg where justice triumphed like that. You saw with your own eyes that such a thing exists. Pass it on, it was promised to us for so long: the dream of peoples – justice. One thousand nine hundred and forty five years after the birth of Jesus Christ: that was the year when world history almost became the Last Judgement.

DAY OF JUDGEMENT

Last night's dream: I'm standing in a barracks yard; I'm still in the army. But now it's called the Federal Army.* Everyone is wearing new, friendly uniforms, bright and attractive, only I am still in my shabby old Luftwaffe outfit from the Russia campaign: worn-out bluish grey, creased, faded, the coat stained; my corporal's stripe is rippled and frayed. I try to grab some new equipment from the clothing store, but I can't get a new uniform. I've annoyed the big shot in charge of the store by addressing him as 'Sergeant'. You ass, he roars back, can't you see that I'm a staff sergeant? Oh, yes, I've got his stars muddled.

I still remember that dream as I drive along Berliner Strasse. Of course you dreamed about the army last night. The war was back. Berliner Strasse is in Frankfurt city centre, running parallel to Zeil. It was only built after the war that destroyed the old town, as a relief road for city traffic, and like so much of our contemporary urban planning it was only half successful. Even before St Paul's Church the traffic starts to block up.

I'm sitting in my car. It's Thursday 27 February, a beautiful, radiant early spring day, on which one should really be driving into the Taunus mountains, into the Spessart, into the Odenwald. A seductive day, bright blue with a silvery sparkle: it will be warm by midday. I've opened the sunroof wide and am trying in vain to light a cigar as I drive. I'm thinking about that dream: What does it mean? It's not true, of course. I'm no longer the corporal in my old uniform. Hitler is dead. My youth is over. So the dream is false. Everybody in this country is wearing new things, sixty million Germans are wearing new clothes, and I'm one of them. The city seems to consist entirely of new things: banks and department stores, shop windows and cars have the cold and beautiful sheen of industrial products. A new era has begun: the era of global technical civilisation. Germany is a developing country within this global civilisation, and Frankfurt is its commercial centre: sober and harsh, beautiful and brutal, a mixture of Old Sachsenhausen and Little Chicago.

I'm driving to the Auschwitz trial. It was in the papers: articles, reports, commentaries, which attracted some attention at first but then provoked only indifference. Later that made way for irritation and displeasure: What is this? It's all so complicated and boring: five years of preliminary research, or so we're told, and a bill of indictment running to seven thousand pages – who's going to grasp, understand, follow all that? It's a matter for experts. It's like a play for the times that was premiered ten years too late: even on the day of its first performance it is out of date. A novel in instalments that has been dragging on agonisingly and fruitlessly for months, a horror novel that bores the public: concentration camp atrocities – who still wants to hear such things, who is still interested? We already know all about it. Obligatory reports in the big newspapers, obligatory reading for nobody, no material for the tabloids, *Bild* wasn't present,* not a topic for parties, and when I recently said in passing: 'I'm off to the Auschwitz trial,' there was a moment of embarrassed, awkward silence amongst the guests. 'Yes, yes, terrible,' someone said in the background. 'You poor thing,' a lady added, and the hostess topped up our whiskies and tried to distract us from this word. I said nothing; there were no Nazis here. I had just used an unsuitable word: people don't like to say Auschwitz after work in our country. The word is taboo.

I'm driving to the Auschwitz trial because I want to see it. I believe that seeing deprives hauntings of their power. Auschwitz is like a haunting. The word has become a strange metaphor: a metaphor for evil in our time. It is redolent of blood and fear and horror, burned and tortured human flesh, smoking chimneys and countless German accountants eagerly recording it all. Auschwitz is like a new verse in a medieval dance of death; one thinks of skeletons, charnel houses, the reaper and the shroud and the new mechanism of death: gas. They say there are no more myths in our enlightened age; but whenever I hear the word I feel as if I am being touched by a mythical code of death in our time: a dance of death in the industrial age, a new myth of administrated death which started here. Doesn't history from time to time bring forth new myths from its womb? Is Auschwitz not in reality Rosenberg's vision: the myth of the twentieth century?*

I'm driving to the Auschwitz trial to understand the myth. I just want to sit there and listen, watch and observe. It's one last chance, now that this wave of political trials has begun again. It's important. It's one last opportunity to meet the past in flesh and blood, to encounter history through its actors, to see the perpetrators and their victims not as projected images of fear or suffering, but as people like you and me. I want to see this contemporary drama before it sinks into the abyss of history. I want to meet my youth under Hitler once more.

After this wave of trials the curtain of time will be closed for ever. The play is over. The plot will become history, it will

pass into the hands of historians, it will provide theses, the-
ories and schools of thought, children will learn it at school,
as reluctantly and wearily as if it were a poem by Schiller:
a subject for the older students, like Pythagoras's the-
orem or Xenophon's *Anabasis*. In two generations it will be
homework for final-year school students to swot up on: Tell
us something about the 1940s in Eastern Europe. And the
examined student will say, hesitantly: There was a big war,
there were the Russians and the Germans and the Poles. And
the examiner, in a slightly sharper tone: What was happening
in Auschwitz at that time? And it may sound as distant and
alien to the examinee as the Battle of the Catalaunian Plains
does to us now. He may not have studied it. Do we have to
study everything in history?

On this bright February day the Auschwitz trial is still
being held in the city council hall in the Römer building in
Frankfurt. The city is noisy, busy and affluent, a bit frantic
and brassy, a lot of Opel Rekord cars, a lot of businessmen,
but this ground bears the curious consecration of history.
The German emperors had been consecrated here from 1562.
A few hundred metres away stands the Imperial Cathedral,
which isn't actually a cathedral since it was never an episco-
pal seat; in fact it is only the parish church of St Bartholomew.
But these few hundred square metres were once – who here
knows this? – the sacred centre of the Holy Roman Empire of
the German Nation.* The coronation records give an account
of the solemn ceremonies as the elect was received at the
portal of the cathedral. They give an account of the coronation mass, the donning of the imperial regalia, the gird-
ing with the sword of Charlemagne. They give an account
of the presentation of the insignia of empire, the proclama-
tion and the seating at the altar of the crowned one. Then
they passed in a solemn procession to St Nicholas's Church

and the Römer, and the exercise of the arch-offices began. A venerable ground on which Volkswagens and Opel Rekords, old Borgward limousines and new Mercedes now battle furiously for space. History has come to an end in a car park.

A small man of pensionable age unsteadily conducts the cars back and forth as they threaten to get stuck in the soft mud, playing at being a car park attendant on his own account. In fact, this huge muddy ground between cathedral and Römer isn't a car park at all: it is just a huge, empty 1960s embarrassment at the weight of history. What should be built there? In 1792, three years after the outbreak of the French Revolution, here in this place where I am now driving around in circles and looking in vain for a parking space, the last German emperor of the Holy Roman Empire was anointed. He was a Habsburg, Franz II, and the day was – what irony of history – also a 14th of July.* Today is 27 February 1964, and inside the Römer they are discussing Auschwitz. It is the twentieth day of the trial.

I feel a little awkward as I climb the steps of the Römer. It isn't Auschwitz that I am afraid of. It is the law. I always feel a certain amount of trepidation at the sight of German prosecutors, judges and police. I continue to have the nightmare of standing in front of a German court again as I did in 1941: Berlin People's Court W, Bellevuestrasse, Floor III, the state vs Broghammer and others, and in the preliminary investigation I was at one point one of the 'others'. Everything was wrapped in blood-red banners with a huge imperial eagle in the middle of the courtroom: three judges and nine lay judges, SS and Party members, and in front of them, in the spectators' seats, political and military dignitaries. Silence, cold, anxiety in the room.

They were German judges passing sentence in the name of the people, German legal staff and German policemen, and since then I find it very hard to bear their hard, dutiful faces, those German peaked caps, the jutting chin, those stupid physiognomies of administrative efficiency. I am always a little afraid of those uniforms. I know it's wrong, one should fight it, we're living in a new state, a better one, but now, as I walk past the group of green-clad police, I feel it again. Now something is bound to happen. Now a uniformed man should step forward and say: Come, defendant, the court has already assembled. But none of them moves. I am no longer the accused – for the first time. I show my press card and another piece of paper from the court, and I hear myself saying, like a stranger: 'I am a German journalist, and I want to attend the Auschwitz trial.' The three green-clad cops fleetingly glance at the papers, put their hands to their caps and then say politely: 'Certainly, this way, two flights up, please', and I enter the building.

There's a wedding going on down in the reception area. People have been married in Frankfurt's Römer since ancient times. This is where the registry office is located: a venerable, famous and popular place for young couples. They are allowed to climb the narrow, cheerful imperial stairs which were built in 1752 and even delighted the young Goethe, up into the ceremony room, and even today, while the criminal proceedings against Mulka and others are being heard upstairs, weddings are celebrated here. Formally dressed young couples sit around on the benches waiting to be called. The new banns are posted in a box on the wall. Witnesses and relatives stand embarrassedly around. A photographer kneels in front of a pair of newlyweds and says: 'Nice and friendly, please', and the bride in her white veiled dress, with a huge bunch of roses in her hand, smiles a little awkwardly. It will become one of those many family photographs, sweet and stiff, that will later stand in faded silver frames on

German sideboards, and in twenty years this friendly young man in his dinner jacket, now shyly smiling at his bride, will probably be a pinched and resigned German civil servant, a bit stuffy and pedantic, and may well hate this woman, and the woman will hate him, and that will be the marriage; a quite normal, proper marriage.

The photographer has just set off his flash. For a fragment of a second the couple stands in the dazzling flood of light as if on a stage: Eros, the marriage festival. And the date will appear on the back of this wedding photograph: Frankfurt, 27 February 1964, and they won't know that on this very Thursday two flights up a Viennese doctor raised his hand to give the oath and testified: 'According to our calculations between two point nine and three million people were killed in Auschwitz.'* And he added: 'So help me God.' Meanwhile downstairs weddings are still being celebrated, rings are still being exchanged, kisses are still swapped and photographs are still taken for the family album in twenty years' time. Is that our life?

I have been sitting here in the courtroom for an hour. After much toing and froing a police officer wangled me into the back rows of seats. The hearing has already been under way for a long time. I'm late – because of the shortage of parking spaces.

And as always when you suddenly walk into the middle of a performance, a film, a play, at first I sit there a bit dazed and clueless and can't find my bearings in the discussion. I sit there and think: So this is it, this is the famous Auschwitz trial. I'm getting a distinct feeling of slight disappointment. I had imagined the scene differently: more severe, more stately, more dramatic, the prosecutors on high chairs and the harassed defendants on lowly benches. I think of the Nuremberg trial and the many television reports from the

Eichmann trial: the man in the glass case.* There had been some grandeur and drama: Day of Judgement, nemesis, tribunal and history's verdict. Where is that here?

I'm sitting in a friendly, medium-sized bourgeois hall in which an investigation authority is obviously holding a meeting. The room is about a hundred and twenty metres long and forty metres wide, the walls are panelled to the ceiling, cheap light-brown wood; on the right a green curtain conceals a stage, and next to it hangs a large relief showing the camp at Auschwitz. Eight lamps that recall the stiff modern style of the 1930s illuminate the high-ceilinged room. On the dominant transverse wall one can see the blue, red and white coat of arms of the region and the city.

There is conventional council furniture in the hall: hulking benches and lighter, modern chairs, and even the faces of the judges sitting beneath the coats of arms emanate a sound sense of civic spirit, a respectful, paternal calm, seriousness and level-headedness appropriate to worthy city fathers. The chair is a small, squat man with a round head, perhaps in his late fifties. He has big mountains of files in front of him and sometimes flicks through them. On either side are the two other judges, one young, the other very old; they too are flicking through files. Over the loudspeaker a voice is heard. I look for the defendants in the room but can't find them. I look for the witness stand but can't see it either. I have a good seat, I have a clear view of everything, but it all seems so strange, so incomprehensible and so confusing to me. About a hundred and twenty or a hundred and thirty Germans are sitting in this room. Citizens of our country, Federal Germans in 1964, and I can't tell who are the prosecutors and who are the defendants. They can't be told apart.

A voice, rather dark and indistinct, comes into the hall over the speaker – it must be the witness's voice – and since I don't even understand who is who I decide at least to listen. And the voice says: 'Birkenau was divided into three parts: B I, B II and B III.' And after a pause: 'And then there was the mysterious section B II b: a mystery in this inferno, a section of Auschwitz in which women and children and men lived together, they hadn't had their hair shorn off. The children were even given milk and had a kindergarten.' And again, after a pause, the voice adds: 'But the bitter end came for them too. Six months after their arrival, the inmates of B II b, over three thousand of them, were suddenly gassed.' And after another pause the voice from the speaker says: 'I shall now describe my own arrival in Auschwitz. I first came to the prisoner of war camp, Auschwitz I. Even before we reached the camp, the SS approached us and asked: Have you got money, a watch? Give it to us. You won't be able to keep it in the camp anyway. Then I'll help you in the camp. Above the gate that we marched through it said: "Arbeit macht frei".* On the left we could hear waltz music; a band was practising. We didn't think that we were entering hell. Everything looked so peaceful, so calm.' The voice pauses again. Now the big hall is very silent. A woman right at the front, a member of the jury, has started to cry. The voice recounts how they were brought to the washroom, how they stood there naked, crammed tightly together, and they didn't know whether water or gas was going to come out of the shower. 'We waited and waited, but nothing happened. The only thing we could do was lick the dripping water. Then we were driven back outside into the open; it was a cool May night, the rain drizzled softly, and we stood and waited, we stood all night. Then, the next morning, we were shaved, but you could hardly call it shaving: our hairs were torn out. And then they said: Now you're going to get your number for depositing your clothes, you have to remember it, it's important for your release. But it was just the number that was tattooed on our skin. Then it was clear to us that we weren't people, but just numbers.'

The voice from the speaker falls silent. The sentences become slower and more halting. There are pauses now, whose silence is audible in the room: pauses of memory for the speaker, pauses of embarrassment for the listeners. It's as if everyone here is gazing into the void; everyone looks shocked and stares straight ahead. Some women have hand-kerchiefs pressed to their faces when the voice continues: 'I could already see the chimneys, I was standing by the doors of the gas chamber when my group was suddenly brought back from the crematorium. Everything seemed mysterious. Only later did we understand: the corpses of a transport from France that had been gassed in the night and hadn't yet been cleared away were preventing the murder of new victims. And later there was another miracle. An SS man came and asked: Are you the doctor? Are you a good doctor? I said: I don't know. He took me away, and so I was saved. After that I became the camp doctor in the quarantine section, and only then did I learn the purpose of the camp.'

And the voice goes on to recount how it slowly adapted to the camp, how it adjusted to it, how it learned to live with the machinery of death. Living for five years in Auschwitz, indeed surviving Auschwitz, doesn't just mean suffering for five years, but also becoming used to it, coming to terms with it, adapting; it means indifference, coldness, even malevo-lence towards the misery of those who were lost.

A frightening recognition: human beings are the product of circumstances. In a city of death everyone is in it together; whether you're giving out bread or gas, you're a part of it. Only those who cooperate in the mechanism of extermina-tion have a hope of survival. An incomprehensible, furious will to survive must have ruled the voice: I won't die, not me,

I'll survive. Despair and desire, just to stay there, just to hold out, to cling to one's bit of bread, eat, drink, obey, work, join in, don't die, survive – survive, so that one day you can bear witness to what human beings did to human beings here. Eventually the day will come, it will take twenty years, it will be 27 February 1964, it will be in Frankfurt, and that time, fulfilling that absurd delusional fantasy from Auschwitz, has come at last. Now is the moment of truth.

A strange state of excitement has gripped me. For two hours I have been sitting here in the Römer and I've become disoriented. It's as if the grid squares of time have been thrown into confusion: which time actually applies here? The time from before? It's war, it's 1943, everything is back as it was then. Winter in the East, war in Poland and Russia. I'm twenty-two again. I was in Vitebsk, in Orel, in Smolensk, bullet-riddled cathedrals and shattered party headquarters in the city centre, further out the small, thatched cottages of the Russian people. There were no men left. They were dead or imprisoned or in Stalin's armies. Women in rags. Rags on their bodies, over their heads, their feet wrapped in big, tattered rags, women trying to sell some rock-hard maize bread or precious salt. I was only a corporal driving a truck, an Opel Blitz, but for these harmless, ragged Russian women I was one of the mighty victors, the green angels of death that they were afraid of.

It is a war winter in Russia, a cold, desolate day in the snowy steppes, the ground frozen hard as rock, it crunches under the snow-chains of my vehicle. I'm driving my lorry from the rear to the front, past endless white forests; you can drive for hours in this huge country without advancing so much as a step. Is Russia endless? Is Russia the world? The engine sings brightly in low second gear. I have soldiers, German paratroopers, in the back, twenty young, healthy, harmless people with machine guns and rifles who some-times curse when we go over potholes and the truck bounces heavily up and down like a seesaw. I'm driving a platoon of paratroopers to the front, to a front that is supposed to pro-tect not only Berlin, but also Auschwitz. I'm from Berlin, twenty-two years old. I've never heard the name Auschwitz.

The witness has just used the word 'Sanka'. I stop short. Sanka – you know that word, don't you? Is it a place name in the East, a medicine? You've heard it before, haven't you? It's so hard to remember everything after twenty years. And while I'm brooding about that strange foreign word I hear the voice saying: 'Most of them were immediately injected with phenol in Sankas.' And the word is suddenly there, it surges up from the shafts of the past: memory of my youth, memory of the technical language of orderlies and batta-lions, the hateful, horrible language of the army to which I belonged: a Sanka was a Sanitätskraftwagen, an ambulance truck, and back then, in the Second Company of the 1st Paratroop Regiment, you drove a Sanka. Of course: they were those nimble little white buses with the red cross on the roof, also Opel Blitzes. The wounded were driven off in them, and sometimes they screamed and groaned and cursed their driver to hell. I drove my Sanka to the main dressing station in Smolensk. Everything was in order. I was just doing my duty like seventy million other Germans. We were all just doing our duty.

But what would have happened if the word on my march-ing orders had by chance not been Smolensk, but that other, unknown, meaningless word Auschwitz? What would have happened? Of course I would have driven my wounded men there too; of course, a soldier always does what he is ordered to do. I would have driven them to Auschwitz, and I might have delivered them to the prison doctor who is speaking here as a witness: every day one or two wounded men for the hospital barrack in Auschwitz. That's not a lot. And then what? What else would I have done? I could hardly have failed to notice that what was being done here was not healing but killing. What would I have done? Probably I would, like everyone else, have closed my eyes and pretended for a while that I didn't notice anything. I might have hated my staff sergeant and my platoon leader even more, I might have clenched my fist in my coat pocket and listened to the BBC in the evening. But apart from that?

I didn't volunteer for the paratroopers, I was detailed from the Luftwaffe. And what if I'd been detailed to Auschwitz? In that mad, chaotic time many things were possible.

Why wouldn't one send a corporal unfit for the front to a labour camp in the backwoods? What would I have done? Would I really have been a hero? Would I really have stepped up to my lieutenant and said: 'No, I'm not doing that. Not me. I refuse this order'? I would have gone there as a soldier, as a man in uniform, and would have had the chance to survive, and I wanted to survive – God, yes!

I don't think I would have been able to join in with the murders, the killings, the burning, the sorting. That's a different dimension. But wouldn't I have tried to get out of it somehow, with the many little tricks the soldier knows? Certainly, I wouldn't have been a hero. I would have withdrawn and kept my mouth shut. But who can say for how long? Killing too can become a habit. Everything is habit. If ten thousand people are killed every day, who is to say that I wouldn't have got used to it too after two years?

The window at the back of the hall must have been opened slightly. Street noises rise up from outside, Frankfurt's lunchtime traffic. A tram rattles by. It's the number 18, the one that stops between the Römer and St Paul's Church. I hear the ringing of the conductor's bell, the opening and closing of the doors, the bright hum of the engine and then the carriage rattling down the street. There's something helpful about that moment. The passing tram is a certainty. It exists: a proper, everyday presence, people travelling from Praunheim to Riederwald at lunchtime and thinking about anything but Auschwitz, women with shopping bags and men with heavy briefcases. The squeaking and singing of the tram mingles strangely with the voice from the speaker, which is now talking about children who were thrown alive into the fire because gas supplies were low. 'Otherwise we won't be able to do it,' the instruction had come from above. And they wanted to do it – of course they did. And I feel fear and horror rising up in me. Outside the number 18 goes past, and here inside they're holding the Day of Judgement. And as for me: Where am I? Where do I stand?

I have come as a stranger, a German journalist; I just wanted to be a spectator, but now, as I follow the voice again, I sense that no one here can remain a spectator. The time barriers have shifted, past has become present, the film of life has been rewound and now it's starting jerkily again. And why, in that film, shouldn't there be a picture of me in a moment, showing me surrounded by uniformed men, me in the campaign in the East, and what will I be doing in that picture? Who will I be?

'The session is being adjourned for ten minutes.' I must have been lost in thought for a moment, I hear the words as if delayed and see everyone suddenly getting to their feet and heading for the exits on either side of the hall. And I too rise to my feet like a sleepwalker, I walk absent-mindedly towards the door on the left with everyone now pushing through it, and then I'm standing outside in the foyer and for a while I don't know what to do. It's like the interval at the theatre. The audience grab some fresh air, light cigarettes, stand around in groups and critically discuss their impressions. Some men have gone to the cloakroom and asked the attendant for their coats. Are these the disappointed, the discontented ones, who are familiar with the tragedy and are leaving the play at the interval?

Two older gentlemen in black silk robes, who must be lawyers, are just coming out of the toilets; one of them stops by the mirror and carefully, and perhaps a little vainly, adjusts his tie. The other one has gone over to the cloakroom attendant, he has set down a few coins and asks for a Coca-Cola, and then they both go back into the foyer. The one with the Coke bottle must have made a joke, because the other one suddenly starts laughing uproariously: the broad, stolid faces of the Frankfurt bourgeoisie, the hearty laughter that you hear in Sachsenhausen, tipsy and pleasure-loving. The everyday life of the lawyer – why shouldn't a barrister laugh at break time?

Then someone speaks to me. He's a colleague, I've known him for years, a journalist from Hamburg. He was in a camp himself, and he now starts to tell me about the trial. He's been here since the first day, he knows everyone, and phones in his report every evening to his radio station in Hamburg. He has countless pieces of paper and notes on him, he talks intimately about the judges, the jury, the lawyers and defendants as a theatre critic might talk about a well-known cast. 'And what about the defendants?' I ask expectantly. 'Where are they?' My colleague looks at me with some surprise, smiles ironically, puts his hand to his mouth as if he's going to whisper and says: 'God, man, don't you see them, the one right next to you and the man in the armchair at the back? And those ones over there at the window, and that one by the cloakroom? And so on.' And then I understand for the first time that all these friendly people in the hall earlier, and who I thought were journalists or lawyers or spectators, that they are the defendants, and are of course indistinguishable from the rest of us. Twenty-two men are on trial here, eight are in prison, fourteen out on bail, and with a very few exceptions, they look like everyone else of course, they behave like everyone else, they are well-fed, well-dressed gentlemen advanced in years: academics, doctors, businessmen, craftsmen, caretakers, citizens of our affluent new German society, free Federal citizens who have parked their cars outside the Römer just as I have, and are coming to the hearing just as I am. There's nothing to tell us apart. And suddenly I find myself thinking of the film that I saw shortly after the end of the war. It was called *The Murderers are Among Us.** That was seventeen years ago.

Now a completely new interest has been sparked in me. I'm back again, I'm alive again. I would like to see them, observe them, recognise them. There must be something that tells us apart. It must somehow depress them, single them out, make them lonely. You can't go walking around here with the burden of Auschwitz on your shoulders as if it was a theatre interval. And I cautiously approach the large group of leather seats by the wall. Five corpulent, convivial gentlemen sit there, a bit massive and bloated, drinking Coca-Cola and Sinalco, smoking cigarettes and holding conversations with each other. Gentlemen during a break in a corporate board meeting. Two of them seem to have problems walking; they have with them black walking sticks with rubber ferrules. They must have been through a few things. The oldest, in an impeccable dark blue suit, has a slightly reddish face, his hair is snow-white, and my colleague says: 'That's Robert Mulka, SS-Obersturmbannführer and adjutant to camp commandant Höss. He's now in export in Hamburg. He is staying here at the Frankfurter Hof, and on days when the court isn't sitting he takes the express train to Hamburg to look after his business. The prosecution accuses him, amongst other things, of being responsible for procuring the Zyklon B required for gassing. Of being involved in the selections at the ramp, of being involved in the transport by truck of the individuals selected for gassing to the gas chambers.'

And I stand there speechless, glance furtively over and look away again. I don't want to be intrusive, I don't want to stare at this group the way you stare at strange wild animals in the zoo, and I'm stunned that murderers should look like that, so harmless, so friendly and paternal. But then I realise that these convivial gentlemen are not ordinary murderers, they are not emotional criminals who kill somebody out of pleasure or lust or despair. All of those things are human. They exist. But these are modern murderers of a kind previously unknown, the administrators and functionaries of mass death, the accountants and button-pushers and clerks of the machinery: technicians who operate without hatred or emotion, little functionaries from Eichmann's great empire – deskbound murderers. Here a new style of crime becomes apparent: death as an act of administration. The murderers are pleasant and punctilious officials.

The hall slowly starts filling up again. The policeman by the entrance has given a discreet signal to the public in the foyer, and those who have just been mingling with one another, chatting and smoking as if at a book-fair party, suddenly separate themselves into discrete groups and gatherings, to go on playing their legal roles. Lawyers too always have something of the actor about them.

Suddenly I understand the seating arrangements in the hall. The defendants are sitting right in front of me: four rows, each row six seats deep, leading right up to where the judges are sitting. The eight prisoners enter from the right through a side entrance, accompanied by two blue-uniformed policemen. One prisoner, with a brutal smile on his lips, has just bent down to his lawyer and is talking with him for a while.

The fourteen defendants on bail have also taken their seats; each one has sitting on his right two lawyers with fat yellow ring binders on their tables. In black capitals these bear titles like 'Files 4 Ks 2/63' and next to it, in brackets, 'Auschwitz Complex'. I am strangely moved to see such codes on official files. And the word 'complex' in brackets.

Some things in the hall are clearer to me now. The gentleman right in front of me, whom I tapped on his shoulder earlier to ask him who the defendants were, but who didn't answer, is Schlage, Bruno Schlage, defendant number 8, caretaker and bricklayer foreman, a simple, slightly primitive face, thin crew-cut hair, the pinched features of a German subaltern. The prosecutor accuses him of involvement in the so-called 'bunker evacuations': fetching prisoners from their cells to be shot against the 'black wall': 'The accused is said to have taken part in these shootings.' Sitting right in front of him is an interesting, intelligent-looking face. His name is Breitwieser, he was a lawyer and legal advisor, detailed to Auschwitz in 1940. He is defendant number 13. He looks so likeable and calm that I would have been happy to employ him any time. 'The prosecution accuses him of introducing the poison gas Zyklon B into the basement rooms of Block II, where the first gassings of people were carried out from October 1941, leading to the deaths of some 850 Soviet prisoners of war and some 220 prisoners from the hospital block.' About a thousand deaths, a relatively small figure in the context of this trial, and the defendant may be thinking: But they were Russians, not Jews – weren't they? Today he works as an accountant.

I flick through the printed material handed to me by my colleague from Hamburg, and since the court hasn't yet appeared I quickly skim what it says about defendant Boger: Wilhelm Boger, born in 1906 in Stuttgart. He is sitting at the front, identified as defendant number 3, he is a commercial clerk, another accountant. What is that about? I wonder. Did the whole SS consist of bookkeepers? I always thought they were supposed to be heroes, knights, German men. I skim-read what it says about selections, segregations, gassings, mass shootings and the 'black wall'. These are all crimes with countless victims, mass murders, unimaginable and anonymous. In effect, they don't say much about Boger's particular case, but then I read on: 'Boger is also held to be responsible for many individual actions. Among other things, he is charged with killing prisoner secretary Tofler in Block 11 with two pistol shots; holding a sixty-year-old cleric in the prisoners' kitchen under water until he was dead; shooting a Polish couple with three children with a pistol from a distance of about three metres; kicking to death the Polish General Dlugiszewski, who had been starved until he was practically a skeleton; that in the autumn of 1944 after the suppression of the uprising of the special work detail at the crematorium, he and other members of the SS killed with pistol shots to the back of the head some one hundred prisoners who had been forced to lie down on the ground.' And I go on flicking through the pages and finally read: 'Without being legally registered, after the war Boger spent several years in the region of Crailsheim, where he worked on a farm. He was later employed as a commercial clerk in Stuttgart.'

And I think: So there he was, an upright, reliable book-keeper of the kind that is needed in Stuttgart, a man who you can depend on, a man who readjusted to life, who was able to sleep at night and who certainly had colleagues and friends and a family – the dead made no appearance in his dreams. And if, here in Hesse – 'Red Hesse', as it is known – we did not have this brave and resolute man, State Prosecutor Bauer, a lucky stroke for our legal system, a miracle in the context of our bureaucratic state, and had this same Fritz Bauer not decided years ago: 'We are going to hold this trial, whether it is popular or not, we will hold it here in Frankfurt!', Boger might still be sitting loyally over his commercial lists, drawing lines and dashes and writing sums, in red, blue and green, would still not be haunted by his victims in his dreams. And Mulka, more intelligent, more cultured, older, a former adjutant to Höss and a successful Federal citizen, would still be running his coffee import business, he would be on good terms with people in foreign countries, he would doubtless be a democrat, 'occidentally' inclined, friendly towards the Christian Democrats but not active in the party,* submissive towards the West, harsh towards the East. And when he hears about inhumanity, and you hear so much about inhumanity in the East, then he will always be thinking of the Communists: of Bautzen, Waldheim and Hilde Benjamin – never of himself.*

How, after Auschwitz, can these men become such civil and efficient Federal citizens? How does it happen? What do the doctors, the psychologists, the psychiatrists have to say about that? None of the defendants has become 'conspicuous' again. They have all created an ordered life, a home, a position for themselves once more, they were worthy and respected citizens in their communities, efficient and successful, and often popular. There at the front sits Kaduk, defendant number 10, Oswald Kaduk, butcher and nurse by trade. He has one of the few repellent faces here. He must have been what you imagine a camp thug to be like in your worst nightmares: always brutal, often drunk. The prosecution accuses him of thousands of killings, but here too the small private bestialities, which happened in passing and off duty, so to speak, seem much more telling: throttling, beating, abusing, throwing prisoners against the barbed wire, whipping a hanged man because the rope broke and then hanging him again, putting the rope around prisoners' necks and then kicking away the stool on which they stood, trampling a young Jewish prisoner to death, shooting others in the belly, and doing this over years because it was what Hitler wanted. And the same Kaduk came to West Berlin in 1956, he became a nurse under Willy Brandt's city government, and his patients still report in letters to this Frankfurt court that he was a good, warm-hearted carer. 'Papa Kaduk' was what they called him in the hospital.

Again there is that horror within me: so is that human? Is that what human beings are like? Or is there perhaps regret, atonement, inner change, the death of the old Adam? The way Kaduk is sitting up at the front next to his lawyer, broad, massive and confident, a fat, short-necked butcher type who is cleverly representing his case, that's not the impression he creates. And if he hadn't been fetched from his hospital one day, he might have died in Berlin at the age of seventy or eighty, an elderly and respected citizen of the city, who would have received his pension and some kind of medal of honour, a citizen of the free world.

And now for the first time I understand why there are Jews who won't come back to this second German republic, even though it's become decent and tolerable again. Fear, very private fear: the tram driver, the person behind the counter at the post office or the station, the chemist or indeed this capable nurse from West Berlin – of course, it could have been any of them. You never really know. New York or Tel Aviv are safer, and anyone with deaths to mourn in this country, wouldn't they, mustn't they have this small, private terror of us Germans?

For ten minutes now the voice has been coming out of the speaker again. By this time I know that it belongs to the first witness for the prosecution, the first of a hundred and fifty who will follow. The witness's name is Dr Wolken, he is a doctor from Vienna, an elderly, white-haired gentleman who seems a little stiff and rigid in his movements. He is severely disabled. He too has survived, he too has readjusted, he too has become a citizen of his country with family, friends and colleagues – both perpetrators and victims have survived. Their survival and their confrontation is the premise of this trial. What divides them today is above all the psychology of memory, the mechanism of forgetting. Some want to forget, but they can't. The others are supposed to remember, but they can't. They have forgotten everything, they have just planted radishes and set up kindergartens and played sport. I don't know which is more painful: remembering or forgetting. Freud taught that guilt can never be forgotten, but only ever be repressed, and that repression leads to neuroses and compulsions.

But is Freud right when it comes to Mulka and his comrades? Where are the neuroses? And is bringing things out into the open, is expressing things, really salvation? Is it not a new torture of experience? Again I hear the voice: 'A group of ninety children came and spent several days in the quarantine camp, then lorries arrived, on to which they were put to be driven to the gas chambers. One of them, a slightly older boy, called out to the children when they resisted: Just get on the truck, stop shouting. You've seen how your parents and grandparents have been gassed. Up there we'll see them again. And then the boy turned to the SS men and shouted: But don't imagine that you're getting this for nothing. You will perish the way you're making us perish.' And the voice on the speaker continues after a pause: 'He was a brave boy. At that moment he said what he had to say.'

It is a painful moment. The clock says it's eleven thirty-seven. But is that really the correct time? Does it not stand still here for an instant? It's one of those moments when the court ceases to be the court, when the walls open up, when it becomes the tribunal of the century. It's no longer about these many little villains, these Mulkas and Bogers and Kaduks. Here history is being attested to, history is being written, stock is being taken, testimony given of the dance of death in the twentieth century. The actors of this terrible play are gathered here, the perpetrators and the victims, they are to see each other here, testify to how things were, they are to tell the world what happened. And this too had happened: 'There were a lot of naked women there, who were beaten on to a truck after a selection and then driven to the gas chamber. We were mustered in front of the barrack, and they called over to us men, hoping that we could help them … after all, we were their natural protectors. But we just stood there trembling, we could not help. Then the trucks passed, and at the end of every column came the truck with the red cross. But it was not carrying patients, it was carrying poison gas.'

I look around the courtroom: everywhere there are embarrassed faces, downcast silence, German shock – at last. The journalists sit on the left and write along as if under a spell. Up on the left-hand side of the gallery sits the public, between a hundred and twenty and a hundred and thirty people, densely packed, who stand in a queue in a side street here every morning, even before eight o'clock, to get the few tickets. Who are they? What Germans would come here of their own free will? There are good, hopeful faces, a lot of young people, students and school pupils, witnessing, with bewildered faces, a spectacle put on by their parents. Their parents? Surely not, certainly not theirs, but certainly other people's parents. There are also a few older faces there, sixty- or seventy-year-olds who have clearly not come here out of a craving for sensation. What is missing up there is my generation, the middle generation, which it concerns, which was there. But they don't want to know anything more, they already know everything, they're familiar with it, they now have to work at that time of day, they have to make money, they have to keep the economic miracle going. He who looks back is lost.

Sitting to my right are three nuns, girlishly slender and prematurely aged. They must be those Protestant sisters from Darmstadt, the Sisters of Mary, who have now, after the war, come together to form a religious community. They want to atone for the Christian sins against Judaism, and they always send some sisters here so that they know what they should be praying for – it's the style of a new, modern church. Are the Sisters of Mary praying right now for the naked women on the truck? Do prayers help here? Do court rulings and sentences? What can possibly help here? I don't know, I have no idea, I just know all of a sudden that I really am at the Auschwitz trial now, and that it was a good idea to come.

Because that's how things will go on now: for weeks, months, maybe years. Hundreds of people will come from America and Israel, from Canada and England, all the scattered children of this dead city will assemble, stone by stone, a mosaic of horror from their tiny prisoners' world, they will open a labyrinth of guilt that no one can escape. This labyrinth will be terribly confusing and will cruelly destroy all self-righteousness, all arrogance and benefit of hindsight. There will be witnesses here who come to speak up appreciatively, even gratefully, for SS officers. That happened too. There were some wearers of the death's-head insignia who behaved fairly and bravely and said: I'm not doing that. They were acquitted soon after the war on the basis of statements from prisoners. And there were inmates, imprisoned for their politics, who came to power in the camp, who became prisoners with official tasks and beat, tortured and killed more people than some men in uniform. For example the gentleman to my right: Bednarek, businessman Emil Bednarek, not an SS man but a victim of Hitler, who stands accused here, as a political prisoner and block elder in Block 8, of torturing fellow prisoners to death. 'In many cases he is said to have forced prisoners of the punishment battalion to stand under the cold shower until they developed hypothermia, stiffened and fell over.' A victim of Hitler now looking for victims of his own. 'Then the defendant is said to have dragged them into the courtyard of the punishment block, where they lay during the night, so that most of them died. In the summer of 1944 the accused is said to have distinguished himself when, during the liquidation of the family camp B II b he, together with SS officers, beat some Jewish prisoners who resisted being transported to the gas chamber. As a result at least ten inmates lost their lives.'

And the charge sheet against Emil Bednarek, who now owns a shop and the railway restaurant in Schirnding, continues. A victim of Hitler who himself murdered others. That is the maze of Auschwitz. No, there is really little truth in the rumour that this trial was an excuse for a new wave of de-Nazification, that it was a belated quest to find scapegoats, to take belated revenge on the SS, to carry out a witch-hunt against minor Nazis. The question of political views and organisation is not raised here at all. It is all about murder.

Here Jews too could become criminals, and individual members of the SS resistance fighters.

For the camp is not only a political nightmare, it is also a social reality: a parallel world with new hierarchies and privileges and new forms of oppression and favouritism. You come to the camp for some reason; but once you're there you belong in that new second world, in the unique order of the camp in which you can rise again or fall according to new laws. And who wanted to fall? I think of film footage from the Warsaw ghetto: there you saw Jews, emaciated Jewish policemen with armbands, beating their fellows with clubs and hoping that this might win them the favour of the SS, who didn't want to get their hands dirty. In Germany too there were Jewish councils which were reasonable, conciliatory and insightful, and which were still saying to the members of their community in 1938: You've got to understand, it's understandable, after all, we must register, we are Jews, after all, it doesn't mean anything. And I hear of trials in Israel where Jews are being convicted even today because they were the most feared thugs in the camp. Today, here in Frankfurt, at number 87 Unterlindau, a lawyer and notary has his practice who once was an SS judge, and when he came to Auschwitz and saw that it was hell, began to indict the torturers one by one. His name is Dr Morgen, and he will give a statement later in this trial, but even today it is clear that this SS officer had the courage to bring SS men in Auschwitz to trial. They were given sentences of up to twelve years. This man is even said to have brought a case against camp commandant Höss in Weimar in 1943, although it came to nothing of course. A subject for Ionesco or another absurdist playwright: SS judges bringing cases concerning prisoner abuse in Auschwitz – infringement of the Führer's edict. Prison sentences are delivered, and at the same time

the crematoria burn brightly day and night – no infringement of the Führer's edict. But no, it's not a contemporary
drama of the absurd. That was the reality in those days.

Lunchtime. Several times now the chairman has glanced
at the big public clock, which shows the time as just before
half past twelve. Lunchtime, food time, time to go home; all
over Germany people are putting aside their work and sitting
down to steaming soups, cabbage stews, roast meats, washed
down with beer. That will happen here too – of course. 'The
session is adjourned until 2 p.m.,' I hear the chairman say,
and everyone takes a deep breath. They all get to their feet,
suddenly they are all in a hurry. Everyone wants to get to
their car, their tram, their seat in the restaurant or their couch
at home, a holiday from Auschwitz, two hours' dispensation
from history – just to get out of that ghostly maze and back
to some of the tangible, harmless reality of this country. Now
what matters is the place in the queue for the cloakroom,
people push and shove, still somewhat in a state of shocked
distress as if after a good stage play, hurrying down the corridors with their coats flying.

Walking ahead of me is Breitwieser, the intellectual-look-
ing accountant with Zyklon B experience. He walks quickly
and with a spring in his step, although he limps slightly on
the stairs. Where could he be off to? For a moment I wonder
about following him, observing him, seeing what car he gets
into and who he shares his lunch break with. I think: How
will he appear among the other Germans? Will they notice
him in the restaurant when he sits there and eats? Will he
stand out in any way? Someone should check. But then I
know it would be fruitless. People with Zyklon B experience eat and sleep and live in this country like everybody

else. They are contemporaries, they share that sick German era of ours.

Strange to find one's way back now. All of a sudden nothing of what you heard earlier rings true any more; you're in the present now, it is 27 February 1964. The sun shines brightly on the Römerplatz, there's a spring-like warmth and it's as sunny as it would normally be only in Milan or Turin at this time of year. Tourists stroll with their cameras across the bumpy Römerplatz and take a few pictures as they pass. 'Lovely,' an old lady beside me says. A group of black tourists show some interest in a fountain, marvelling at fragments of the Middle Ages, the marvelling of tourists, thirty seconds long. A half-timbered house from 1383 greets them in the background, it is freshly painted: the famous number 1 Fahrtorhaus, the oldest building in Frankfurt. Surely you must love this homely, dreamy, poky Germany. James Joyce and Thomas Wolfe once stood in this square too, while Hitler ruled Germany – intoxicated and spellbound by German gothic architecture.

I look across to St Paul's Church, I step into Paulsplatz, and all of a sudden I face the furious, rushing lunchtime traffic of a living German city. It's like a hurricane of technology; I find myself lost in it. Now you can't think about shooting and gassing, of chimneys and crematoria, you have to make sure you cross the street safely. It's deadly dangerous, it's like a civilised jungle, a battle of machines, long queues of cars, signals, signs, green lights and red lights and the yellow blink of cars turning right, policemen waving their arms like puppets. We shove each other and push and wait, and someone shouts something at a driver who didn't pull away quickly enough on a green light, and taps himself on the forehead. That's how it is. That's Frankfurt at five to one, the commercial centre of free Germany, that's the Federal Republic every lunchtime. And all the car drivers seem to belong to my generation, men in their mid-forties who are now playing at war in the street, in the shop, on the stock market. This is Germany, its other, second, efficient side. You can't think about Auschwitz. They'll run you over. They will kill you right here on the zebra crossing in front of St Paul's Church.

I escape into a side street. Suddenly paralysed by melancholy I creep past walls. Here too there are tall, new buildings, but then it grows quieter; big, well-tended bookshops appear, and all of a sudden a tall, brown patrician house with bull's-eye panes, tiered storeys and cast-iron doors reminds me that I'm on Grosser Hirschgraben: the birthplace of German classicism, Goethe's house. Two buses, American sightseeing coaches, park in the narrow street and spit out tourists who quickly want to treat themselves to the Germany of philosophers and poets. They will fall into this trap, I imagine: Goethe's comb and Frau Rath's frying pan, all rubbish, all fake. Goethe's house was destroyed in the war, it was burned out. Goethe and classicism are finished in Germany. It made perfect sense that this house should have been reduced to ashes in the worst year of Auschwitz.

Later I sit in a little Romanian restaurant not far from Goethe's house. An elegant stillness. Only nine or ten tables, along the wall a long buffet with exclusive hors d'oeuvres, muted music in the background. The owner comes over in person, an elderly white-haired gentleman from Bucharest, and, with a lot of bowing and a bit of French, recommends the specialities of the house. And I think: What is it with us Germans? Are we again the masters of Europe? The peoples that only yesterday we invaded, looted, oppressed and wanted to turn into a race of slaves are tripping over themselves to please us, to serve us. They should hate us, despise us, they should keep out of our way whenever they can, but they don't.

They come to us, millions of foreign workers live in our country, and millions of Germans go on holiday to their countries. Does that mean we've become a new, better people?

I open the newspaper, nervously scan the headlines and read: 'Erhard discusses European politics',* 'No transit passes for Easter weekend', 'The negotiations with Bulgaria', 'The Argoud case before the Bundesrat',* 'Too much gold'. Hang on, did I read that correctly? Was there something about too much gold? And then I start reading the article: 'West Germany's money managers are complaining of a situation that almost every government in the world devoutly wishes were the case: once again, large amounts of gold are accumulating in the vaults of the Bundesbank.' I go on reading and discover that today, 27 February, gold supplies are running at 30.3 billion marks. 'The Federal Republic estimates that over the past twelve months over 2 billion marks in foreign capital has flowed into West Germany. Twenty-five per cent of all German loans this year were made to foreign borrowers.' And I wonder again: What is it with this new Germany?

And since my food is probably going to be some time, once again I bring out the notes that I took during the witness statement. I've only been writing down words, the words of the witness Dr Wolken, not SS words, but words from the victim, the language of the camp. I read: 'Detail, introduce, liquidate, load, gas, die, select, prepare material, treat corpses arising, to the gas chambers, women's camp B I, Zyklon B, the ramp, take away, intercept, transfer, move, muster, play sport, run, shoot, transfer, pour water, musical band, waltz music, dog unit, hare-hunting, beating, death record, transfer Muslims, put Muslims in carriages, kill Muslims, injection to the heart, foot on the small of the back, hop ...'

As I skim these words, all of a sudden I understand the dream I had last night. Of course, it's the language of my old uniform, it's the word 'Sanka' that you couldn't remember. That language is still alive, it still exists, it's being revived here in Frankfurt. We can put on as many new uniforms as we like, put on as many golden clothes as we like. The staff sergeant who shouted at me and refused me my new uniform is of course Hitler: he still exists within us. He still rules us from the darkness, from the underground; somehow he has created a fissure within us all. Some go chasing after money, others go to the Auschwitz trial, some cover things up and others expose them again – two sides of the same German coin. That Hitler, I think, he's going to be staying with us – for our whole lives.

AFTERWORD:
TEN YEARS LATER

I wrote this book in the winter of 1964–5; it was published in 1966. Did I really write it? Did it not write itself? It was a beginning, a start, a first attempt at self-liberation. Such beginnings, particularly when they occur in advanced years, always have something violent and explosive about them. They come as if dictated. There is compulsion involved, an unconscious dynamism, to free oneself at last from a heavy burden. The burden is called the past, youth, childhood trauma: a very personal and at the same time a political story. At first you don't want to write. You want to escape from some unbearable systemic pressure. The strange thing about literature is that such attempts at saving yourself save others at the same time. In this sense *The Broken House* is unquestionably a success. It was welcomed by both critics and readers. Apart from a few voices on the extreme right and left, it received nothing but accolades.

The book has its own origin story, which, looking back today, deserves to be mentioned. It was not actually planned. It wrote itself, almost unexpectedly, back to front. In the mid-1960s I moved from Baden-Baden to Frankfurt am Main. I was emerging from a long period of silence, of inner uncertainty and professional subordination that had become oppressive towards the end, in order to begin the life of a freelance writer. It was a time of expectations, of curiosity, of hopes for me. At the time Frankfurt offered a great deal of material for critically engaged contemporaries. Among the people that I met here was the chief state prosecutor of Hesse – who has since died but remains unforgotten – who was preparing the Auschwitz trial at the time. Fritz Bauer became a friend and invited me to the trial. I sat in the courtroom as a mute witness for four weeks and then wrote, originally for the magazine *Der Monat*, a report on the trial which, slightly expanded and rewritten, now forms the final chapter of *The Broken House*.

It was only afterwards, in the autumn of 1964, that my own memories began to rise to the surface. When a writer is sitting in on a trial – can he identify with anyone but the defendant? This psychological process may seem absurd given the monstrosities of the Auschwitz trial – but it was still at work. The bestial acts under discussion here could not keep me from asking the question: So what about you? How would you have behaved if you had happened to enter the bureaucracy of these death camps as a lowly soldier? Are there born murderers? Are they not all produced by society? What would you have accepted in silence? How guilty would you have been? Of course, there is that murder threshold. But where exactly would you have drawn the line? So, in retrospect, the trial was a process of self-examination; it was also directed at myself.

Critics have praised *The Broken House* for the moral radicalism of its approach. In *Die Zeit*, Marcel Reich-Ranicki called it 'a book about Germany without lies'. If this is the case, I realise now that it is precisely because of its ruthless, indeed self-torturing, act of identification with the world of the defendants. I didn't exclude myself, I didn't keep myself out of it, I went beyond outrage, I felt the compulsion to question my own past. There was really no National Socialist demon to be found in this adolescent from a petit-bourgeois Berlin home. On the contrary, in the context of his limited possibilities, he had always withdrawn from such things; indeed, he had some unmistakable if helpless acts of political resistance to show. But was that all there was? Guilt and atonement aside, were there general abnormal attitudes that formed the preconditions for Hitler's dictatorship in Germany?

I started to remember. I followed the trail, I penetrated the past, I returned to my youth and childhood. It was, so to speak, my first experience of travel: travel into my own past. I found what I went on to develop in the first chapter, 'A Place Like Eichkamp'. I rediscovered my parents' house, my youth under Hitler, which was a quite atypical, unique youth. Precisely because there was no guilt to expiate, because my family and I had never fallen under Hitler's spell, there was an ideal, complex-free field for self-analysis. I discovered what I had not previously really been aware of: the phenomenon of the apolitical German lower-middle class, which in its social insecurity, its instability and its hunger for irrational solutions provided the fertile seedbed for National Socialism's seizure of power within Germany.

It was in this way, step by step, that the four central chapters covering my development to the end of the war came to be written. Another chapter which was supposed to describe my wartime experiences as a German corporal between 1941 and 1945, and which would logically have belonged between 'The Arrest' and '1945, Zero Hour', never quite worked. Time in the army and the war occurred to some extent outside of my first-person experiences. I have never really been able to make them my own, at least not so far. The critical reader will see a gap here, which I admit.

Instead, the theme of the family came ever more dominantly to the fore. In the process my parents' house became, almost unintentionally, a metaphor for Germany. The title, which I chose deliberately, and which some readers called into question, is precisely my subject: I'm not talking about a shattered, destroyed, divided house – it's broken by inner corruption, just as 'the collapse' in Germany happened not in 1945 but in 1933, from within. To that extent, the chapter 'A Requiem for Ursula' is the key to the whole subject. What is being described is the biological self-dissolution of a German family, something that cannot be described in purely rational terms: the process of its inner decay, its unconscious sympathy with death. My sense of myself as the last one, as the only one, which I believe is also apparent in my later books, comes from that. It has never abandoned me, it continues to define me. Of course the friendlier, more productive phrase also applies: the last ones are free. It's in that freedom that I live today.

Books, as we know, have their own destiny. By the time the public is starting to engage with them, the author has usually moved away from their attendant problems, because he is liberated. This has been true since the days of Goethe's *Werther*. You write about suicide not in order to kill yourself but to keep on living. You write about the end not in order to die but to find a new beginning. That's how it was in this case. I felt liberated after finishing the manuscript. Over the years that followed I tried to engage in my writings with my surroundings and current events – critical analyses of the Germany of the late Adenauer period, the German Democratic Republic, the division of the German people – and later with 'Foreign Fatherlands', to quote the title of one of my books. Travelling into the world with the baggage of that past: I don't want to decide here whether this should be seen as an expansion of horizons or, as is some-times observed, a flattening out of the original intention. I have never seen these two 'forms of travel' as contradictory. Both were necessary and compelling stages in my devel-opment. You can only find yourself as a writer if you open yourself up to the world. But you can only open up to the world if you have previously come to terms with yourself. This book retains its importance in my life as a document of self-cleansing, of the spring-cleaning that runs through all of my work. Its key sentence right at the end: 'That Hitler, I think, he's going to be staying with us – for our whole lives', is still valid and demonstrable in my present-day writings. To that extent I think I have remained true to *The Broken House*.

Of course ten years later one can see the strengths and weaknesses of such a debut more clearly. It inevitably bears all the features of a *Sturm und Drang* production. It draws its persuasive power from a primitiveness, a naivety in its ques-tioning, of a kind that you only have once in your life: right at the beginning. Subjectivity dictates. The dominant tone is one of adolescent defiance, which keeps my distinctive ironic style in the background. Viewing it in psychoanalytic terms, one might speak of an anally aggressive engagement in the phase of defiance, but such formulations, however psycho-logically accurate, contribute little to the illumination of the events described. Still, on some pages I sense a sharpness to the engagement which, as for example in the picture of my parents, borders on injustice, indeed on lovelessness. There are some things that I would today relate in more differ-entiated form, and with greater psychological nuance. The narrative process is often determined by an emotional sense of drama which is not entirely free of a certain exhibition-ism. The narcissism that lies behind this, the tendency to self-enjoyment, is still unreflected, entirely naive. Today I would try to introduce it deliberately and ironically into the narrative process. Even after ten years, the language has an intensity that still seems fresh to me. Sometimes however, by today's standards, it is too direct, too massive, too wood-cut-like in its simplifications. There are some things that I would represent in a more complex way if I were writing today. That would make the book fairer, but it would also certainly make it lose some of its passion and vitality. That pain is a powerful source of direction for the writer, but not a sufficient one, seems apparent to me on every page when rereading the book today.

At the same time this painful beginning brought so much social reality to the surface that the new edition of the book, which had fallen out of print ten years after its first publication, seems sensible, indeed politically imperative. The generation of those who were onlookers, participants, adversaries, at any rate contemporaries of Adolf Hitler, is beginning to thin out. The time will come when there will barely be any eyewitnesses of those twelve years. What could be taught and learned from this era is still served up in many historical works and schoolbooks. But what happened between the murderous boulders of history which were moving at the time, in terms of private failure, human behaviour and social climate, cannot be captured in history books. The human-background fresco of an age needs personal memory and literary representation. Unchanged by the developments of the last ten years, I confess: the book contains authentic news from a Reich which, though vanquished long ago, must never be forgotten. It contains the experience of a generation, which may be helpful to those who come after, if they want to know what it was really like, that business with Hitler and the Germans. To that extent the words that Wolfgang Koeppen wrote when *The Broken House* was first published still apply today: 'Krüger's look back in rage and grief could and should become a German handbook in the good and traditional sense that someone has written down and preserved what happened to a people.'

I have looked through the text for the new edition. Apart from some references which were contemporary at the time and are no longer, I have changed nothing.

Horst Krüger
Frankfurt am Main, March 1976

GLOSSARY

page 2
Founded in 1898, the *Morgenpost* was Berlin's most popular newspaper.

page 4
Published in 1906, Georg Hermann's novel *Jettchen Gebert* tells the story of a Jewish family in 1830s Berlin; Hermann's books were blacklisted by the Nazis and the writer would be murdered in Auschwitz in 1943. Paul Lincke's *Frau Luna* (Mrs Moon) and Johann Strauss's *Die Fledermaus* (The Bat) were popular operettas; the overture to Emil von Reznicek's comic opera, *Donna Diana*, was frequently performed in concert halls and on radio.

page 5
The German playwright Bertolt Brecht and the Soviet film director Sergei Eisenstein transformed theatre and film in the 1920s, through artistic innovation and political partisanship.

page 7
Arnold Zweig, author of the anti-war novel *The Case of Sergeant Grischa* (1927), decided to leave Germany on 10 May 1933, the night his books were burned by Nazi students in Berlin and elsewhere. Of Jewish descent, the writer and theatre critic Ludwig Marcuse too was forced to flee the country in 1933. Although

classified as a half-Jew, the poet and novelist Elisabeth Langgässer decided to remain and only narrowly escaped deportation. The Swiss National Public Radio transmitter at Beromünster was the only German-language radio station to provide criticism of the Nazi regime and its propaganda. The Nazis regarded Beromünster, like the BBC, as an enemy radio station, and listening to it became a punishable offense.

page 9

Paul von Hindenburg, head of the Imperial Supreme Command in the First World War and Germany's president from 1926 to 1934, and Alfred Hugenberg, media tycoon and leader of the German National People's Party (DNVP), were figureheads of the nationalist right.

page 10

Ernst Thälmann was the leader of the German Communist Party from 1925 to 1933, when he was arrested by the Nazis; he would be executed, on Hitler's personal orders, in Buchenwald concentration camp in 1944. The author of *Buddenbrooks* and winner of the Nobel Prize in Literature, Thomas Mann was one of Germany's most famous writers. When the Nazis came to power in 1933, Mann and his family emigrated first to Switzerland, then to Czechoslovakia and finally to the United States.

On 30 January 1933, Germany's president, Field Marshal Paul von Hindenburg, appointed a Cabinet of National Concentration, under Hitler as chancellor, that consisted of politicians of the nationalist right. Hitler's coalition partners believed that they would be able to contain Hitler and curb the worst Nazi excesses. That evening the Nazis celebrated their Führer's appointment with torchlit parades.

Black, white and red had been the colours of the flag of the German Empire, which came to an end in 1918; black, red and gold were those of the democratic Weimar Republic which succeeded it. Initially, the Nazis restored the imperial colours to be flown alongside the swastika flag but from 1935 the latter became Germany's sole national flag.

page 12

On 21 March 1933, a historic meeting took place between Hindenburg, Germany's First World War hero, and Hitler in the Garrison Church in Potsdam, symbol of Germany's Prussian heritage, on the occasion of the inauguration of a newly elected Reichstag. For many Germans the 'Day of Potsdam' seemed to mark the beginning of a national renewal; in fact the ceremony had been carefully orchestrated by Joseph Goebbels. With the passing of the Enabling Act two days later, the Reichstag and German politics were firmly under Nazi control. 'The good comrade walking by your side' is a reference to the popular soldiers' song of the First World War, 'Ich hatt' einen Kameraden'.

Götterdämmerung (Twilight of the Gods), the third part of Richard Wagner's *Ring des Nibelungen* tetralogy, refers to the Yggdrasil of Nordic mythology, the ash tree that represents the entire cosmos.

page 14

The *Deutsche Allgemeine Zeitung* was a conservative national newspaper; the *Lokal-Anzeiger*, the local advertiser. The *Völkischer Beobachter* was the official newspaper of the NSDAP.

The pompous, vain and incompetent Hermann Göring was the butt of many jokes in Germany.

For those on the left, the Social Democrat politician Gustav Noske became notorious for quashing the uprising of the radical left in January 1919 with the help of nationalist militias, the Freikorps, resulting in the murder of the Spartacist leaders Karl Liebknecht and Rosa Luxemburg; he served as Germany's minister of defence from 1919 to 1920. After the abdication of the emperor in November 1918, the Social Democrat Friedrich Ebert became the German republic's first chancellor, before serving as its president from 1919 to 1925. Philipp Scheidemann, another

Social Democrat, famously proclaimed Germany a republic on 9 November 1918; he served briefly as chancellor in 1919. Heinrich Brüning, of the Centre Party, was the Weimar Republic's chancellor from 1930 to 1932, during which time he controversially relied on presidential emergency decrees to push through policies dealing with the consequences of the Great Depression. He was succeeded by the conservative politician Franz von Papen, who was instrumental in bringing Hitler to power in January 1933.

page 17
Sauerbraten is a traditional German meat dish, deriving its name 'sour roast' from the fact that before cooking the meat is marinated for days in a mixture of vinegar or wine, herbs and spices.

page 23
Formed in response to the collapse of the empire and the revolution of November 1918, the German National People's Party (DNVP) was the major party of the nationalist right, refusing to recognise the democratic republic and its institutions. From the late 1920s it lost its influence, and many of its voters, to the Nazi Party. The two parties frequently worked together, and the DNVP supported Hitler's appointment as chancellor in January 1933.

page 24
In October 1933 the Nazis introduced the Eintopfsonntag: on the first Sunday of every month, German families were to forgo their Sunday roast and eat a frugal one-pot (Eintopf) meal or stew as a sign of national solidarity. The money thus saved was to be donated to charity. Volksgemeinschaft, literally the 'people's community', was the Nazi term for a German ethnic community defined by racist criteria.

page 25
The actress Emmy Sonnemann's 'powerful husband' was Hermann Göring.

On 29–30 June 1934, in the so-called 'Night of the Long Knives', Hitler removed the leadership of the SA, which was accused of plotting the overthrow of the Führer, as well as some of his prominent critics among the conservative elites. Some 200 people are thought to have been executed during the purge. The SA leader Ernst Röhm's homosexuality was publicised in a campaign to discredit him.

page 26

In the Concordat concluded with the Papacy in July 1933, the Nazi regime promised to protect the integrity of the Catholic Church and its lay institutions; in return the clergy would abstain from any involvement in German politics. While it marked the end of political Catholicism, the Nazis soon violated the agreement in their attempts to curb the influence of the Church in public life. In a concerted campaign, the Catholic press was harassed; Catholic Youth organisations were dissolved and their assets confiscated; and Catholic priests and monks were prosecuted for sexually abusing children and teenagers, as well as for breaking foreign-currency regulations. In their pastoral letters Germany's Catholic bishops spoke out in protest against the repression.

When in a sermon in August 1941 the Catholic bishop of Münster, Count Clemens August von Galen, openly condemned the killings of tens of thousands of mentally ill and disabled people in German hospitals and institutions, Hitler ordered a halt to the 'euthanasia programme', although the murder would continue in less conspicuous ways.

page 27

When Germany's emperor, Wilhelm II, was deposed in November 1918, he went into exile in the Netherlands where he lived at Castle Doorn until his death in 1941.

page 28

Anschluss describes the German annexation of Austria in March 1938, after the Wehrmacht had invaded the country; for many

Germans and Austrians it was the country's long-desired 'return to the Reich'.

page 29
One of the largest beer halls in Munich, the Hofbräuhaus served as a venue for Nazi Party meetings and rallies in the 1920s.

page 31
Philemon and Baucis are a poor, old couple in Ovid's *Metamorphoses*, who offer hospitality when the gods Jupiter and Mercury visit earth in disguise and are rewarded for their humanity and piety. In his play *Faust*, Johann Wolfgang von Goethe transforms the classical story when he has Mephisto murder the old couple because Faust covets their home and land.

page 38
The French pharmacist and psychotherapist Émile Coué (1857–1926) promoted positive auto-suggestion as a method of self-improvement, centred on the repetition of the formula 'Every day, and in every way, I am becoming better and better.' Alfred Karl Brauchle (1898–1964) was a prominent promoter of homeopathy in Germany; Hitler made him a professor in 1943. The Austrian philosopher Rudolf Steiner (1861–1925) was the founder of anthroposophy. Helmut Fahsel (1891–1983), a Protestant convert to Catholicism, was one of Germany's best-known writers and public lecturers on religion; critical of the Nazis, he emigrated to Switzerland in 1934.

page 46
As Reich Minister of Science, Education and Culture, Bernard Rust headed the ministry in which Krüger's father worked.

page 48
Hans Grimm's 1926 novel *Volk ohne Raum* (A People without Space) provided Hitler with the concept of 'Lebensraum': the living

space required by the German people for their existence, which had to be secured through the conquest of territory in the east.

page 48

The sixteenth-century saint Teresa of Ávila occupies a central place in Catholic spirituality and mysticism; Thérèse of Lisieux, a French nun popularly known as 'The Little Flower of Jesus', is one of the Catholic Church's most popular saints. Therese Neumann, a peasant woman in the Bavarian village of Konnersreuth, claimed to have had her eyesight restored, and various ailments cured, by Thérèse of Lisieux, when the latter was beatified in 1926. She also developed stigmata and reported visions of Christ. Despite being denounced as a fraud, she remained the focus of popular piety. The Nazis were concerned about her popularity and she was kept under surveillance by the Gestapo.

page 54

In Bertolt Brecht's play *Saint Joan of the Stockyards*, a contemporary Joan of Arc becomes a martyr in her fight to alleviate the suffering of the poor in the meat-packing plants of Chicago, exposing the workings and manipulations of capitalism. Although written in 1929–30, the play was not performed until 1959, when it premiered in Hamburg.

page 65

Neues Deutschland (New Germany) was the official newspaper of East Germany's ruling Socialist Unity Party (SED).

page 68

Walter Flex was a German writer whose novella *Der Wanderer zwischen beiden Welten* (The Wanderer between Two Worlds) reflected his experiences as a volunteer in the First World War; he was killed in 1917. His romanticism and idealism made him popular with teenagers, while his glorification of war led the Nazis to style him as a nationalist hero.

Industrialist, statesman and public intellectual, Walter Rathenau was instrumental in the organisation of the German war economy in the First World War. In 1922 he was briefly the Weimar Republic's foreign minister. The first German Jews to attain such high political rank, he was assassinated that year by an anti-Semitic, right-wing terrorist organisation. While Rathenau became a martyr to German democrats, the Nazis suppressed all memory of him.

Kaspar Hauser was a teenage boy who arrived in the city of Nuremberg in 1829 and claimed to have grown up in total social isolation in a darkened cell. Hauser's story and the truth of his claims remain shrouded in mystery; but in the popular imagination he became the archetypal feral child.

page 74
Friedrich Nietzsche's *Thus Spoke Zarathustra*, Friedrich Hölderlin's epistolary novel *Hyperion* and the poetry of Rainer Maria Rilke were popular reading for many middle-class boys coming of age at that time.

page 83
As first secretary of the East German Communist Party, the SED, from 1950 until his death in 1971, and as head of state from 1960, Walter Ulbricht was the de facto ruler of the German Democratic Republic.

page 100
While in German the informal 'Du' is used to address children and adolescents, family and close friends, the use of the formal 'Sie' and 'Herr' (Mister) is a sign of courtesy and respect in communication with acquaintances and strangers.

page 101
Friedrich Schiller (1759–1805), Johann Gottlieb Fichte (1762–1814), Novalis (1772–1801) and Wilhelm Heinrich Wackenroder (1773–98) were key figures in German Idealism and early Romanticism.

The poetry of Rainer Maria Rilke (1875–1926) and the novels of Hermann Hesse (1877–1962) were popular with the young searching for a spiritual connection with the world.

page 102

Untermenschen, or subhumans, was a racist term used by the Nazis which denied humanity to Jews, Slavs and others, thereby legitimising their exploitation and destruction.

page 117

Mathias Wieman was a popular German actor on stage and screen; Elly Ney was a pianist famous for her performances of Romantic works.

page 120

Fortress Europe was a propaganda term used by the Nazis to describe a continent under German occupation, which had to be fortified and protected from Allied invasion.

page 121

With its themes of heroism, betrayal and sacrifice, the medieval Nibelungen saga, revived by Richard Wagner in his *Ring Cycle*, was a key component of the ideological repertoire of the Nazis. Nibelungentreue, the loyalty of the Nibelungen, in particular was evoked in the final phase of the war to appeal to the German people to make sacrifices for Reich and Führer.

page 122

Arnold Böcklin (1827–1901) and Anselm Feuerbach (1829–1880) were popular Romantic painters whose work often portrayed scenes from classical mythology, with particular focus on death and mortality.

page 130

Alfred Weber was an economist and sociologist of culture; in 1933 the Nazis forced him to retire from teaching at Heidelberg

University. Karl Jaspers trained as a psychiatrist but turned to philosophy and is regarded as one of the key proponents of existentialism. As his wife was Jewish, he too had to give up his professorship in 1936 and a publication ban was imposed on him.

Martin Heidegger was one of the most influential philosophers of the twentieth century, in particular through his interpretation of existence – Dasein, or 'being there' – in *Being and Time* (1927). He joined the NSDAP in 1933 and served as the rector of Freiburg University in the first year of the regime. In recent years the publication of his 'black notebooks' has revealed the extent to which Heidegger embraced Nazi ideology and anti-Semitic views. 'Turn', or Kehre, describes the perceived shift in his thinking from ontology to language and poetry.

page 134

Hitler committed suicide in his Berlin bunker on 30 April 1945. His appointed successor as head of state, Admiral Karl Dönitz, negotiated Germany's capitulation with the Allies. The German Instrument of Surrender, marking the end of the Second World War in Europe and the demise of the Nazi regime, was signed on 8 May.

page 141

Established in 1955, West Germany's democratic defence force, the Bundeswehr, or Federal Army, was conceived in its ethos in a deliberate break with the traditions of German militarism.

page 142

Bild was and remains Germany's most popular tabloid newspaper.

page 143

Alfred Rosenberg was one of the Nazi Party's chief ideologues. His book, *The Myth of the Twentieth Century* (1930) mixes politics with religious mysticism in celebration of 'the myth of the blood', the racist agenda with which the Nazis were redefining the century. In Rosenberg's use of the term, 'myth' means essential truth rather than fabrication or falsehood. Despite selling more than a million copies by 1945, the book seems to have been little read; even Hitler claimed to have read only a small part, disliking its pseudo-religious tone.

page 144
The Holy Roman Empire of the German Nation comprised an array of kingdoms and principalities in Western and Central Europe. Its origins lie in Charlemagne's coronation as emperor of the Frankish lands in 800, but its focus began to shift onto the German territories with the coronation of Otto I in 962. A loose and decentralised monarchy, its emperor was chosen by mostly German princes-elect and crowned by the pope. It was dissolved by Napoleon in 1806 when the last Holy Roman Emperor, Franz II, abdicated.

page 145
The storming of the Bastille on 14 July 1789 marked the beginning of the French Revolution, which would depose of France's hereditary monarchy.

page 147
Historians now estimate that at least 1.1 million people were murdered in Auschwitz.

page 148
In a highly publicised and televised trial, Adolf Eichmann, one of the key architects of the Holocaust, was tried in Jerusalem in April 1961. During the proceedings he sat in a bullet-proof glass booth to protect him from assassination attempts. He was found guilty of all charges, sentenced to death by hanging and executed on 1 June 1962.

page 149
'Arbeit macht frei' – work sets you free – was the cynical slogan displayed over the entrance gates of a number of Nazi concentration camps.

page 156

Released in October 1946, *The Murderers are Among Us* was one of the first German films made after the war. It tells the story of a former military doctor, traumatised by his wartime experiences, who meets again his former superior officer, now a successful businessman, who had ordered the killing of more than a hundred Polish civilians, and brings him to justice.

page 160

The conservative Christian Democratic Union (CDU) was in government from 1949 to 1969.

Hilde Benjamin was an East German judge and minister of justice who presided over numerous political trials; in 1950 she participated in the so-called Waldheim trials, when the Communist authorities tried 3,400 alleged war and Nazi criminals. Bautzen in Saxony was a political prison, run by the Stasi.

page 170

Ludwig Erhard was West Germany's chancellor from 1963 to 1966. In his previous post as minister of economic affairs from 1949, he had been the architect of Germany's post-war economic miracle, the Wirtschaftswunder.

In February 1963, the French army officer Antoine Argoud, who had been convicted in absentia for attempting to assassinate French President Charles de Gaulle and lived in hiding in Munich, was kidnapped by French intelligence and taken to France. The Bundesrat is the upper house of the German Parliament, which represents Germany's sixteen federated states.

Compiled by Jörg Hensgen

penguin.co.uk/vintage